Find Your Place and
Breathe for the
First Time

*Overcoming the Things and
People That Haunt You*

GARY WEINSTEIN

FIND YOUR PLACE AND BREATHE FOR THE FIRST TIME
OVERCOMING THE THINGS AND PEOPLE THAT HAUNT YOU

iUniverse books may be ordered through booksellers or by contacting:

iUniverse
1663 Liberty Drive
Bloomington, IN 47403
www.iuniverse.com
1-800-Authors (1-800-288-4677)

Because of the dynamic nature of the Internet, any web addresses or links contained in this book may have changed since publication and may no longer be valid. The views expressed in this work are solely those of the author and do not necessarily reflect the views of the publisher, and the publisher hereby disclaims any responsibility for them.

Any people depicted in stock imagery provided by Thinkstock are models, and such images are being used for illustrative purposes only. Certain stock imagery © Thinkstock.

ISBN: 978-1-5320-3029-1 (sc)
ISBN: 978-1-5320-3031-4 (hc)
ISBN: 978-1-5320-3030-7 (e)

Library of Congress Control Number: 2017915679

Print information available on the last page.

iUniverse rev. date: 04/02/2018

Important Notice

The concepts, insights, and recommendations included in this book are not intended to, in any manner, take the place of seeking professional care.

If you are feeling at risk of harming yourself or another—or you believe that someone else might be at risk of harming himself/herself or others—you are urged to seek out law enforcement assistance and/or mental health care.

Why I Wrote This Book

I wrote this book after many years of talking with so many people who—on the most basic level—were struggling with who they were and who they wanted to be. They were trying desperately to come to terms with what they felt were their limitations, weaknesses, and failures. Everything they did and felt was overshadowed by relentless uncertainty and searching. After a time, it became evident to me that when there was not a solid understanding and foundation of personal value and independence, everything else in their lives was tainted. The result, too often, was chronic frustration, pain, helplessness, and hopelessness.

The one common thread in virtually all those situations was that the people were searching outside of themselves for validation, value, and direction. Ultimately, they were searching for someone, or something, to give them purpose, comfort, and safety. In other words, they wanted value. It was only when they looked inside themselves for value and validation, they were finally free to make wise decisions, focus on their own goals and dreams, and accept their mistakes, flaws, and weaknesses. Only then would they be propelled forward.

It was only when they freed themselves from the punishing opinions and influences of others, that they could clearly see the path that was right for them and those they cared about. People need to recognize what is already there. You have value, and you can create your own vision according to your own values. Without tainted influences, perspectives, and perceptions of others, you can avoid unhealthy, destructive, counterproductive practices, and follow your own path to your dreams. It is too easy to lose sight of this vision and too easy to assume things will never be better.

I wrote this book to help readers create a vision of life that is free, focused on the future, active, dynamic, and rewarding. This book provides the tools to reach that vision.

Contents

Appendices

Introduction

We get one chance at life. There are no practice shots or do-overs. There's no extra credit for good intentions. We have only one chance. And the most exciting of questions; "How far can my life take me?" … can all too quickly be replaced with the most despairing of questions; "Where did my life go?" Life passes so fast that, before we know it, what once were dreams of our future, if we are not vigilant, can quickly become disappointments of our pasts.

This book is about not losing sight of your dreams; not being distracted, beaten up, put down, or talked out of what you want, or who you want to be by the people and things that haunt you. It's about not giving up. It's about knowing yourself and being happy—perhaps for the first time—with who you are.

There had been so many long nights playing and replaying scenes from the prior day that turned into days long since past. Each sad or bad event soon became magnified and haunting. Each happy event soon became tainted, and then it was turned into nothing more than a new basis for self-beating. Every day became a time of measuring and weighing every word, every action, every decision, and every look that crossed her path. Life soon became a series of blows, things to regret, things to loathe, and things from which to hide.

A wrong job decision, a humiliating experience … seven years earlier, a failed relationship, a disciplinary notice, fear of not being accepted, a nebulous feeling of meaninglessness, a feeling that she should be doing something. But what? A feeling that she is not as good or as successful, as she should have been. Frustration, confusion, anger, anxiety, and fear—whatever. It was always after her.

The incessant gnawing that she felt deep in her belly, and the weight hanging heavily about her heart caused her breath to become short and her heart to throb loud and fast. This became an all-to-familiar experience. The resulting frustration, self-consciousness, insecurity, anxiety and self-deprecation were relentless. And in the event, if for some inexplicable reason, they did subside for a few blessed moments, she found herself actually searching for the torment again. "There must be something wrong because I am not in pain. Let me find the pain again. I know it's here somewhere."

No matter what she did, or where she went, she never could seem to find a place where she belonged. She wanted a place where she could find comfort, have value, be safe, and succeed. Where she was okay. Where she could breathe for the first time.

Your mistakes, embarrassments, disappointments, flaws, rejections, regrettable decisions and failings, and the ways others react to you, can destroy your self-esteem and your self-confidence. They can keep you from maximizing your experiences and enjoying your life. They can keep you from focusing on your future, and they can keep you from growing and enjoying that growth. Ultimately, they can keep you from finding your place.

This book was written to help you when you are haunted by your fears, failures, or successes. It is here for you when you are suffering from low self-esteem, or thoughts of inferiority. It is here for you when you are feeling lost, incomplete, empty, lonely, stressed, anxious, confused, or indecisive. It is here for you when you can't find a comfortable position, or a place for yourself. It is here for you when you are your own worst enemy. It is here for you when you are waiting for the next bad thing to happen. It's here for you when you evaluate your life and your value according to the things that have gone wrong in your life instead of the things that have gone right. It's here for you when you can't think of anything that has gone right.

Ultimately, this book is about bringing real change—positive change—into your life, and finding that place you can call your own.

A place where you can find focus, comfort and meaning, no matter who you are, where you are, what you've done, what is going on in your life, who you are with, what you are doing, or how well you are doing it. It's about finding a place where you can feel safe and be safe. A place that will give you an anchor, a direction, protection, confidence, energy and wisdom, all of which to craft and meet your future.

Particularly in a world that has grown so large, moves so fast, and has become so technological. In a world where the human being has become, comparatively speaking, so small ... it is not difficult to understand how you (or any of us) might lose yourself amidst the chaos. Ultimately ... losing your place.

How nice it would be to no longer be controlled, bothered, intimidated, hurt, angered, frustrated, or frightened by the myriad negative events and people in your life. But instead, to learn how to simply consider them, understand them, learn from them, respond to them, grow from them, and then move on and succeed, according to your plan—not someone else's. How nice it would be to avoid some of them, entirely, in the first place.

That's what we will accomplish with this book. My goal is not to talk you out of the possibility that you, or someone else may indeed feel, you're in some way substandard or that you have made mistakes. Instead, this book will help you realize that—when all is said and done—it will be okay; that the things you've experienced, and the feelings, opinions and actions of others, or even your own, will not define you, and will not stop you from growing, improving and moving ahead with your life on your own terms—not someone else's. You can, and will overcome challenges, grow, succeed, enjoy life, and find your place.

My goal is to give you the tools you need to set your life in motion toward success, accomplishment, security, growth, and satisfaction.

By reading this book, you will...

- identify your dreams (if you have not done so before),
- hold on to your dreams (and not lose sight of them),
- not give up,

- find comfort in who you are (and not be repulsed by it),
- look the world in the face (and not hide from it),
- have the courage to do what it takes to win,
- have the courage to risk losing,
- have the courage to start again,
- have the courage to lose again and then start again, and still be all right—and finally win,
- enjoy what's right with you and be okay with what's wrong with you,
- overcome the things—and people—that haunt you,
- find healing when you are broken,
- accomplish the things that are really important to you,
- find your place, and
- breathe (maybe for the first time).

This book is made up of forty-nine tenets that provide the basic guidelines, rules, and tools of thought and action that will ultimately recreate your ways of processing. They will provide you a framework with which to interpret and respond to life's events in a manner that will free you from incessant negative thoughts, emotional pain, and behaviors that haunt you (whatever they may be). These rules and guidelines will clarify things and put them back in perspective. They will guide you to take action and help you accomplish the things you want to do. These rules and guidelines, along with the accompanying thoughts, perspectives, and insights, will take you to new heights. They will take you to a place where you can breathe (perhaps for the first time).

I urge you to read this book in its entirety without practicing, or trying to implement any of the concepts. Do not judge them, go out of your way to support them, doubt them, or test them. Just read. I purposely wrote this book to be an easily read, practical resource, so it can be read several times. After you have read it once, read it a second time. This time consider each concept, as it pertains to you and your life. Then read it a third time, and practice. Read the book often. Write notes in the margins, underline, or highlight key passages, and fold down the corners of pages that particularly resonate with you.

Every time you read this book, the messages will gain strength in your conscious and your subconscious. You will feel the power and learn to design your life the way you want it to look. If a certain concept or situation does not pertain to you, consider its message anyway. You will still gain insights into yourself and others.

This book is written for you—and to you. Throughout this book, I am speaking directly to you. If certain descriptions do not fit how you think, feel, perceive, or respond, simply read on. But before you dismiss a concept as not relevant to you, I urge you to take a careful step back and check again.

We may not be fully aware of what we are doing and why. We may not want to admit that we are doing something that is actually hurting us. Don't be afraid to admit that you have room to improve, or make changes. We all do—every one of us. It does not mean you are defective. It means you are human and have the courage to look at yourself and embark on a new path.

Insight is only part of changing. It takes action and then repetition, and it takes looking at an idea from multiple angles and chewing on them before things actually begin to change.

As you read this book, consider each concept along with whatever is going on in your life. Consider each event in your life within the context of the ideas you learn about in this book. The interplay between these two processes will take you from despair to elation, from failure to success, and from victim to victor.

Watch out for denial. Do not be afraid to keep your eyes open to your positives and your negatives. They all will help you as you read this book. Do not to settle for surrender. While giving up may seem to be the only viable option or it may seem safer, and you might think it is better to be safe, but unfulfilled. Safe, but sad. Believe me, it isn't! You may think changing, or bettering your life is not possible—believe me, it is!

If you're not careful, the directions your thoughts and assumptions take you, can lead you to places you do not want to go. You have to be willing to stop and take a step back and reconsider your long established perspectives, principles, habits and assumptions about yourself, your life and about others. If your basic definition or perception of yourself or your life situation and potential is negative, and you have little confidence in your being able to be successful, then not trying or not trying too hard, may actually feel safer, and why? Because of the assumption that you can't fail at something you don't try, or that it's a lost cause so you can't win no matter how hard you try.

Don't fall into that trap.

It may be a subconscious decision. You may not realize you stopped trying, or are not trying hard enough. You may feel like you have been trying without knowing your efforts are self-defeating. Keep vigilant.

If you feel like your life is carrying you along a preordained negative or hopeless path—or if the book's content is not resonating with you— stop and take a step back. Take a walk, play some golf, read the paper, or watch a movie—and then come back to the book and the issue that is challenging you. But, be sure to come back to it!

If your basic view of yourself, or your situation is negative to the extent that you felt compelled to buy this book, I can't simply tell you to stop thinking negatively about yourself or your situation, and expect you to do so. If you could do so that easily, you would. So, what I'm saying is this: If you do feel basically negatively about yourself or your situation, don't try to force yourself to stop. Instead, be open to considering new insights, perspectives, and responses. It will take you far. It will take you to your place, and it will allow you to breathe (perhaps for the first time).

Remember, you might find yourself saying, "What's wrong with me?" "Why is my life like this?" "Why does this always happen to me?" "Why do I do what I do?" Don't blame yourself when you have questions like these. There is no reason to beat yourself up. We all live our lives in the best way we can. While there may be people out there who want to see you fall on the sword by having you beat and blame yourself over and over again, doing so does no one any good. It is a waste of time, and it is not your obligation. However, what you are doing about it is your responsibility and it is your responsibility to change, if that is what you want to do. No one else can, will, or should do it for you. You have to make the change. This book will help you do just that.

One last point. Don't let back-steps derail you. They are part of growth. You will find glitches, moments where you get hit hard. Moments where you fall back into old patterns of thought. But the tenets of this book will reduce the back-steps, take away their energy, lessen their impacts, and move you past them far more quickly and with much less pain. Finally, this book will show you how to grow and energize from each and every one of them.

With that said, let's start our journey together.

PART 1

Events of Your Life

We all look for a place where we can live our lives with confidence, satisfaction, meaning, safety, serenity, focus, and growth—our own place. You are no different. But getting there has to start with understanding the basic makeup of your life (the building blocks and events).

Chapter 1

Life Events

*W*e often assume—consciously or subconsciously—that the years, months, weeks and days, in fact the moments, of our lives are parts of one long ongoing event. In these cases, it's too easy to treat everything that happens to us during those periods as one long event. The result of this assumption and the resulting assumption is that it is very difficult, sometimes seemingly impossible, to see that we can stop the trends of our lives at any time in order to change directions, or start again.

The fact is, life is a series of completely separate, relatively short events. Although they can be influenced by past events, they are not cemented to them. They are distinct and have definite starts and definite ends. Therefore, once one event has ended, an opportunity to start a completely new event arises. The message, here, is that you can choose to start over at any time. You can change moods, activities, choices, perspectives, priorities, responses, directions, plans, goals, or reactions at any time. These adjustments, in turn, are capable of changing your future. And one single change can significantly change the rest of your life

Example: A man who has just been fired (the first event) can choose to start a positive new second event by walking out of the boss's office and focusing on finding a new job. Or, he might let the emotion of the initial event carry over and he may, instead, go to the nearest bar and start drinking to excess, thereby getting even more depressed. In that second scenario, what was actually a completely separate event (the aftermath of the termination) was treated by the man as if it was a continuation of the first.

Treating your life's many separate events like one single event, fusing multiple events together, perhaps even over the course of your entire lifetime, gathers emotional momentum and will carry you along like the rush of a flooded river carries a tree branch, chews it up and spits it out on the desolate river side. It will do the same to you. The momentum resulting from this perspective can rush you past all your options. You might not even be able to see the options, or see that new events are possible. These are events that can change the direction of your life entirely, so you can start again.

The examples are endless. Take the man who buys a car "as is." He's told, and is led to believe that the car is a good deal. He drives away and the car breaks down a week later. He takes it to a repair shop, but is told that the car is beyond repair. He goes back to the seller and demands his money back. The seller refuses, stating that the deal was final and the car was knowingly bought "as is." The man starts yelling at the top of his lungs and knocks the seller to the ground. The police are called, and he's thrown in jail.

It is important to recognize each new event and that each new event has new opportunities for change. Even before you are able to identify specific possible changes to the events in your life or changes in yourself, it's important to recognize each event, and that each event can make change possible.

In the example of the car buyer, the man experienced the entire situation as one long event, so he let his anger drag him, quite literally, into jail. If he had been able to separate the situation into individual events, he would have been able to stop himself after the seller refused to refund his money. He could have recognized that encounter as the end of an event and objectively determined the best possible next event. Perhaps he would have contacted his attorney, the owner of the dealership, or the Better Business Bureau. Or he might have written a letter to the editor of the local newspaper, describing his experience. He might not have let his emotions and his next actions, resulting from the strong momentum of the perceived single, long, negative event, drag him to jail.

Another example is when you are called in to see your boss. He says you screwed up the project because your report contained inaccurate information. The result is that your company lost the biggest sale of the year. You know that the inaccurate information came from your boss, himself. You remind your boss that he gave you that information. Your boss says that you must have misunderstood him. He claims that is not what he told you.

This is the end of one event. The next event starts with your response. At this point, the flow of energy is extreme and you are being pulled, quite forcefully, toward defending yourself by arguing with your boss. Your anger is already at the exploding point since it was not the first time your boss had done that. The point is not whether you should explode, quit, let it go, or smack him. The point is that you must know that a new event starts here—and you have choices about what you are going to do, or say. You, therefore, have some control over how the situation will progress, and what you'll do next. Therefore, you have some control over what your future will look like.

The following is an example where you actually do make an error. You are driving pre-occupied with the many things on your list of things to do. You run a red light and you hit another car. It is plainly your fault. There are many witnesses. People are calling out, yelling, "What were you thinking? You shouldn't be behind the wheel!" You're feeling bad enough when here comes a police officer. He gets out of the car and grills you for what seems to be an hour. He ends up writing you a ticket. Next, the owner of the car you hit walks up to you and says, "I just bought this car yesterday. You'll be hearing from my lawyer." When he walks away, you turn around and see reporters from the local newspaper and television station just waiting to get at you.

You feel horrible. So many people yelling. You feel two inches tall. By the time you walk away, you are exhausted. You are overwhelmed by all the critical input and insults you received, and you are neck-deep with emotions that range from humiliation, to defensiveness, to fear, to self-loathing, to anger.

These examples illustrate the capacity to drag you away from the place where you can find strength, comfort, control, energy, focus, self-acceptance, success, and growth.

Breaking Down the Situations

Remember, what appears to be one long event actually is most often a situation comprised of several events. To reduce negative energy, gain some control, respond from a position of strength, make good decisions, reduce the negative impact, and get past it all, first break down the situation, as soon as possible. Break it down into definable, time-limited, manageable events. The key is to slow down the situation in your mind to the point where you can, first, step back and recognize each individual event, its start and its end. Second, look for the opportunities to change an existing event, or select a new one. Third, select one, and fourth, make it happen.

In the case of the auto accident, the first event occurred just prior to the accident when you were driving down the street. The second event was the accident—the physical impact of the two cars. The third event was the time between the moment of impact and the first encounter with another person while you were trying to regroup in your car. The fourth event was the response of the other people. And the fifth event was your response to them.

When you are being attacked, you have four response choices (new events): Attack those who are attacking you, defend yourself from their attacks, let the attackers chew you up, or acknowledge the accident and your responsibility (not the blame) for it, and respond to it from an objective position of ownership and strength. Then, learn from it, adjust, and move on.

The key point is that once the event of the accident is over, your response starts a new one. Decide, which new event will serve you best. Now, some people like to lay blame and expect to see displays of remorse, and there are certainly times when remorse is appropriate and needs to be made public. However, remorse should be limited to being genuinely sorry that you did, or said something that caused harm (if, indeed you did). But, that remorse should not involve self-beating, or traumatizing yourself over and over again. You can be sincerely sorry without getting stuck in it. Be sorry, but then move on (even when others try to keep you from moving on by not accepting your apology, by continuing to beat you, by bringing up the event again and again, or by not giving you credit for taking responsibility).

Adjusting and Controlling Events

All events can be adjusted, or controlled in some way, either before or during the event. No event can be changed after it's over, but you can adjust its impact, or your response to it. In this case, you could respond to the fourth event in a variety of ways ranging from shrinking back completely victimized by the others, to attacking them physically. An effective response might be to respond assertively enough to take responsibility while maintaining a level of control, self-respect, and focus. You can keep yourself from being victimized by—and stuck in—the event. Consider the example of an assertive response below:

Car owner: What were you thinking?

You: Like I said, I'm very sorry and I will pay for the damages.

Car owner: You sure as hell will. You shouldn't be driving at all. You don't know what the hell you're doing.

You: (Speaking calmly but assertively) Look, I realize your upset and I don't blame you. I said I'm sorry, and I meant it. I said I'll pay for the damages, and I will. But I won't just stand here while you abuse me. Here is my insurance information.

Pivotal Events

Pivotal events are events you can adjust while a situation is occurring. They may be new events you can initiate to change or reduce the negative impact of an event that has passed, or events you can initiate to counter a pending event that is apt to have a negative impact on you. Pivotal events are events you have some control over. Once adjusted or initiated, these events can change the course of the situation—or the course of your life. Your goal is to identify possible pivotal events. Then select the one you feel will best lead you to where you want to be. Then focus only on that one.

Consider this example: You come home late without calling your spouse first. Your spouse gets angry and accuses you of being inconsiderate since you both are due to be at a party a half hour ago. You lash back that you were running the errand that your spouse had asked you to take care of after work. Your spouse yells back that you still should have called. You storm out. One event. Right? Not right. Actually this was a situation made up of several events, and at any point, you, or your spouse could have taken advantage of the end of any one of them, in order to start a more positive event—a pivotal event—and generate a different, more positive outcome.

Let's identify the events. First, was back when you were asked to run the errand. Second, was when you ran the errand. Third, was when you walked in the door. Fourth, was when you were accused of being inconsiderate. Fifth, was when you lashed back. Sixth, was when you stormed out.

In this example, there were several potential pivotal events where adjustments could have been made. During the first event, you might have stated that you would be late coming home due to the time it would take to run the errand. During the second event, you could have called when you were running the errand to remind your spouse that you would be late. During the fifth event, you could have taken a breath and instead of lashing back, you could have explained that you thought your spouse realized it would take extra time to get home. During the sixth event, you could have chosen to leave quietly to give you both time to step back. Any of those adjustments could have changed the situation dramatically.

Here's one more example: Your company goes bankrupt and you are accused of mismanagement since there is money missing. The community is being flooded with news stories about your apparent incompetence and illegal activities. The board doubts you. You're worried about supporting your family or going to prison. You are overwhelmed and frightened.

Your best chance of survival is to break down the situation into distinct events and identify the pivotal one. Are you going to adjust an event that is happening now, or initiate a new one that will redirect, rectify, or improve the impact of one that has passed?

You might go on the offensive and put your own explanation in the newspaper. You might offer to make things right if you have indeed erred. If you are bound for prison, you might focus on preparing your family for the emotional and financial challenges ahead.

Keep in mind, the pivotal event you want is the one that will best change the course of the situation for the better. Beware, there are those who would try to keep your events connected, treating them as one long event, and not allowing that event to end. They accomplish this by continually blaming you, or relentlessly trying to punish you. This could make it difficult for you to see an end to the negative event and start a new more positive one. If you are still haunted by something that happened either days, months, or even years ago, then you are treating situations of your life, or your life in general, as one long event. Don't let them tie your events together to stop you from getting past them, and don't do it to yourself either.

It can be a challenge to break down a situation into a group of smaller, more succinct and adjustable events. It can be a challenge to see that an event has ended, especially when your emotions are high. But the challenge is not impossible. Select and adjust the pivotal event and let go of all the other individual events, once and for all. Effectively identifying and controlling the pivotal events in your life—and closing out the others—are essential for finding your place.

In the case of the bankruptcy, stop focusing on what people are saying. Don't focus on going to prison. Focus only on the pivotal event you can initiate or adjust now. That's the one you have some control over. If you feel yourself veering back to one of the others, stop and redirect yourself back to the pivotal one.

Tenet 1

Life is a series of individual events. Each of them has a definite start and a definite end. Once one event ends, you start a new one. You're only bound to a past event if you allow yourself to be. Don't! And don't carry the emotion from an event that has ended into a new one that is starting. Identify each event in a challenging situation, then select a pivotal one to make a positive change. There is always at least one pivotal event. Recognize the power you have to select one and change it.

Notes

PART 2

The Anchors

In order to deal effectively with negative events in your life, you have to identify and understand what they are. However, you also have to understand who you are, your nature, your position, the roles you play, and your capabilities, relative to those events. This is because you are not merely a passive player at the mercy of the events that happen to you (even though it might feel like it). You are the director. But you have to ask the critical life questions.

Asking and discovering who you are, what is expected of you, what you are capable of, and what you should expect of yourself are at some level of consciousness, basic objectives of every human being. This knowledge and the search for these answers are the backdrop, the context, and the foundation of your life. These insights are your anchors that keep you grounded, stable, focused, and strong, particularly when things get hard, when you are hurting, or when you are lost. They help you reach your goals and find your place and maintain it, once you've found it. But beware, while there is great value in asking these questions, there are also risks.

Chapter 2

Your Quest for Answers

*A*sking these questions drives you to search, live, experience, seek satisfaction, and grow. In other words—to find your place. However, risk occurs when you ask these questions at times when you can't make sense of it all, or can't find satisfactory answers. "What am I supposed to do?" "What am I supposed to be?" "Why am I still trying?" "Why am I suffering?" "Why is everything going wrong?" "What's the point?" "Where do I belong?" Questions like these can leave you barely afloat in a sea of confusion, hopelessness, contradiction, emptiness, frustration, and loss.

But the search is worth the trip and it's worth the risk. While, by the time you have finished this book, you will have a much better understanding of your place in this world, your role and your value, you will also know that it's okay to not have all the answers all the time. This is because the value and reward of life is more about the searching, the journey—not so much in the outcome. The journey is more important than the destination. Not knowing actually gives you energy, motivation, direction, focus, and meaning, as well as the ability to adjust, move on, try new things and start again.

The true meaning and value of life is actually found by asking questions and not in finding ultimate answers. It's also true that by the time you're done reading this book, you will realize that your searching is no longer the longing and yearning that breeds pain, frustration and desolation. Your searching, in fact, will become the relished seeking of knowledge, opportunities and experiences. The searching, itself, will breed excitement, energy, focus, and satisfaction.

Being freed of the disillusionment of your searching gives you emotional and intellectual freedom, so you can find many of the answers you seek. You can find out who you are. You can find your true relationship with the world and those within it. You can find your true value and your place, but only if you keep searching.

Searching. It is the first step to understanding that to know who you are requires gaining some understanding of your own nature and your relationship with the world. This is particularly important when you don't have all the answers you are searching for.

Tenet 2

The value and the reward of life is more about the searching than the outcome. The journey is more important than the destination. Celebrate the journey every day. Ask yourself, what you have learned?

Notes

Chapter 3

You Are Imperfect (and So Am I)

*T*he number-one reality on the hit parade is that you are not perfect. Don't be offended—no one is. You are not meant to be, and you do not want to be. This is the third tenet. Remember it. Tattoo it on your forehead. Sew it into your clothing. Paint it in a mural on your walls. Whatever you decide, but remember it. Repeat it, drink it, eat it, and live it. Why? First, because, while your striving for perfection can be a key motivator, failing to reach that perfection can be a key cause of your misery. Second, since attaining perfection is impossible, striving for it creates an impossible goal and therefore an insurmountable dilemma. Third, and most importantly, if perfection is your goal, then you have already failed and you are just waiting for the next time you prove that you aren't.

The search for perfection can be exhausting and devastating, because if you base your value on how close to perfection you are, then anything less than perfect is unacceptable or a failure. The goal of perfection can victimize you by constantly reminding you of your faults and failures. The stress comes from always trying to eliminate, defend, explain, fix, or deny them.

The feeling that you need to be perfect is not uncommon. Most people would like to be perfect, but they recognize that they aren't. But some people believe they should be perfect, and if they're not, then they're nothing. They are obsessed with performing in a perfect manner (as they define it). But they continue to fail to reach perfection because like all the rest of us, they are not perfect. So, they grope for it and often inadvertently sabotage their own efforts in the process as they become more desperate for it. They make rash decisions, pushing themselves (and others) too hard, climbing over others, sometimes damaging or destroying them in the process. They may take shortcuts because they think doing so will get them to perfection sooner. But that breeds rashness, and often results in disappointment.

The problem with demanding perfection is the relentless expectations and the stress that comes with it. When perfection does not occur, people become more and more intolerant of the shortcomings of themselves and others, often beating themselves, or others, to a pulp.

Why is perfection a goal? Because to many, perfection is assumed to be synonymous with value. For them, it becomes the most important thing. They feel like they must be perfect. If they're not perfect, they feel like they are nothing. This can be devastatingly self-destructive.

There is one more point, here. If perfection is your only acceptable goal, then you cease to consider the value of the process which is the journey, and it is only your focus on the process that can lead you to the outcomes you are looking for. Consider, if your goal is to have a million dollars and you focus only on the money, or having the money, it will never happen. You have to focus on how to get it. That is the process. That is the journey. Instead of trying to be perfect, learn from every step you take towards perfection, and from every instance that asserts you aren't. Enjoy every step along the way. Every step is growth, and growth is always your goal. If your goal was to have a million dollars, wouldn't you be okay with having half a million, or even a quarter of a million? You could continue to strive for more, but would you feel bad about the quarter million you did have? I doubt it. You'd throw a party. I know I would.

Be careful, though. Even though you might know and assert, intellectually, and consciously, that perfection isn't possible, and that you do not expect absolute perfection from yourself, emotionally and subconsciously you might still be demanding it of yourself and beating yourself up when you're not. Ask yourself: "Do I, in fact, demand that I be perfect?" A sure sign is if you often beat yourself up after you've made a mistake, or have been unsuccessful.

Tenet 3

Allow yourself to be imperfect. Your goal is to learn and grow from your imperfections, not to avoid them. Remember, your focus is on the process—the journey. Strive, not for perfection, but for opportunities to grow. Further, you need to recognize that failure does not impede growth. It is not the opposite of success. Failure fosters action, which fosters growth, which in turn, fosters success. Finally, a failure does not indicate a lack of value. A failure is merely an event with a start and an end.

Immediately, after a failure, which is merely a negative event, plan and initiate the next event, the next step, and the next leg of your journey.

Notes

Chapter 4

Bad Things Will Happen to You

*T*he second reality is that bad things will happen to you. Sometimes things will go wrong—no matter what you do, or how hard you try to avoid them. This is true for all of us.

The key is to anticipate the bad things and accept that they can be others' fault, your fault, or no one's fault. Regardless, don't look at these bad things as foreign intrusions that are descending upon you from some outside mysterious, or not-so-mysterious, force. Instead, look at them as natural parts of life. They are part of you. They are part of the game.

Tenet 4

The fact is that bad things are not foreign intrusions. They are integral and inevitable parts of your life and necessary for your growth. Learn and benefit from the bad things. Don't be beaten by them.

Beware of the string of bad luck. Don't assume these bad things are one single enduring event that has formed an overwhelming, perpetual, and unavoidable cloud under which you are doomed to walk. They are each a distinct single event with a start and an end. But, if you are experiencing multiple bad things continually, the answer to avoiding them, may be a single adjustment. Look for root causes.

Consider your lens.

Many people assume that many more bad things happen to them than to other people. This is probably not accurate—at least not when considering the larger picture.

There are several possible reasons for this assumption. It has to do with the lens through which they are viewing themselves and those around them. First is the tendency to magnify the bad events in our lives and minimize the good. Second, we don't know 75 percent of the bad things that happen to other people. We only know what we are able to see or what we are told. Therefore, what we are primarily aware of, typically, is not the number of bad things that happen to others, or their severity, but what we actually see others do in response to a very few of them. Third, while we tend to be particularly sensitive to the events we have dealt with, we tend to compare our lives to the lives of others who are not faced with those same events. Therefore, we assume they have fewer bad things happening to them.

For example, the woman who feels terribly lonely will likely be more keenly aware of those who are not lonely, or those who don't appear to be, and not so aware of those who are. She also will most likely tend to be unaware of the bad things that are happening to others. Her assumption is that others are not as lonely as she is. If others are not lonely, then they are evidently much better off than she is. This creates a skewed perception that leads to the assumption that no one else suffers like we do. I am not minimizing the intense pain or the seriousness of anyone's particular situation, but be aware that making strong, universal statements, assumptions, and judgments about others may ultimately haunt you and beat you down, and may not be accurate.

Those who have lost loved ones or limbs or sight have known devastation far beyond that which many ever will. For me to suggest that someone should just will that pain away is cold, simplistic, unrealistic, and cruel. In those cases, the pain is real, especially when the events are irreversible.

At the same time, however, recognizing that even those horrific devastations are indeed part of the human experience, and knowing, as we will see later in this book, that there is life after devastation will help to keep perspective, focus, and strength. After reading this book, you will find that, while some bad things can be avoided, others will continue to occur, but the resulting pain, its duration and its intensity will definitely be less, and its ability and power to destroy or paralyze you and keep you from finding your place, will be substantially weakened and diminished.

Ultimately, it's all about balance. We will talk more about this later.

The Value of the Bad

Consider a man who has never experienced bad things (if you can find him). He has, by definition, enjoyed a great deal of success and happiness, but he will never have the same sensitivity and the depth of understanding of the human experience as those of us who have experienced the bad. The bad is necessary. The bad things are tools we use to help us grow. While quite obviously you will not enjoy the bad, and I wouldn't expect you to strive for the bad, I urge you to make the effort to relish the depth that grows within you and springs from those bad things. Don't be beaten by them. Recognize that the bad things are tools that you can use your entire life to deepen, evolve, experience, strategize, grow and achieve. They are, indeed, part of the foundation that underlies, supports, and strengthens your place.

Tenet 5

Bad things will happen to you at some point, and you may feel like you are owed some good things in your life. However, life doesn't pay up just because you want it to or think it should. You have no natural right to that payment. You aren't owed anything

by life. Why? Because it just isn't how life works. Stop trying to collect. Instead, jump on the back of the bad and ride it. Don't let it ride you.

Why Bad Things Happen

So why do bad things happen to people who are good? Why do bad things happen to young people who have not had a chance to commit significant transgressions? This is important when trying to cope with or respond to bad things that seem to defy justice, logic, decency, and explanation.

Through the years, I have heard several different thoughts on the subject:

- There is no reason. Things happen randomly.
- God is cruel. He lets bad things happen to those who do not deserve it.
- God is not able to stop bad things from happening.
- It's God's plan.

I have yet another idea. I believe that the bad things that happen, especially the very bad, unjust, seemingly random things, are precisely the things that give life its meaning. Without bad things, it would be like playing a game that you could never lose. No matter how much or how little you tried, you would win. The result of this would be that you would stop playing because there would be no point and nothing to work toward. The result would also be that winning, or even playing at all, would hold no meaning whatsoever. Therefore, life would no longer hold any meaning. Motivation would be non-existent. The result—total stagnation of the human species.

So, when a loved one dies, the most painful of losses, and we say, why? Somewhere deep inside we need to realize that while the death is horrible, there is, indeed, a point to it. There has to be loss—sometimes an excruciatingly painful loss—in order for there to be meaning in life.

We may still ask, "Why did it happen to my child? Why not someone else's? Why not someone who has had the opportunity to live for many years? Why not someone who deserves to die?"

The answer is that our loved one, like everyone else, was part of the total human experience and as such, had the same chance of being lost. It appears random, but it is part of the design. The idea that something bad can happen to anyone—something that just makes no sense at all and seems absolutely unjust—is part of the design that actually gives life its value and meaning. All of this motivates us to work hard and be vigilant, creative, and cautious. It also motivates us to try to improve the living experience and reduce the chance of loss. This is all in order to live the safest, best and most meaningful life we possibly can, according to our priorities and preferences. So, the next time you suffer a loss, dig very, very deep, and try to find some modicum of solace in the fact that your loss creates the meaning of life. Believe me, I know this is a difficult thing to do in the midst of severe grief and it may take some time. It may never feel completely acceptable. However, know that it is true.

So why isn't the reality of life, that if we live good lives, we won't suffer and if we live bad lives, we will suffer? Wouldn't that create motivation to live good, full lives? It would only work up to a certain point. There has to be an element of complete uncertainty in order to keep us growing, searching, thinking and deepening.

Notes

Chapter 5

You Are Free at Your Core

*T*he third reality is that every human being, deep inside, has a core. Your core is the foundation of your identity and your value, both of which are free and invulnerable to all things and to all people. This invulnerability cannot be lost, destroyed, damaged, penetrated, berated, stolen, inhibited, compromised, injured, or altered by anyone or anything. That core keeps prisoners of war strong and steadfast despite years of captivity and torture. That core gives an actor the courage to go back on stage after a humiliating performance. After a catastrophic business setback, that core spurs a business owner to start again. That core keeps people going when they have suffered the loss of a loved one. That core keeps people who are dealing with a terminal illness functioning and enjoying life as best they can. It is your core that gets you back up after any excruciating humiliation, disappointment, loss, injury, illness, or failure.

Your Core Is Your Identity And Your Value

The sixth tenet provides you the confidence to face, with a sense of strength, those external events and influences that you perceive as threatening, devastating, disappointing, humiliating, frightening, or frustrating. Because, when all is said and done, your core is still intact—no matter what happens to you, what people say or think about you, or what people do to you. It is that part of you which will continue to exist and thrive no matter what the outcome, no matter what your disappointments are, and no matter what you endure.

The core is your identity and at its center lies well protected, your value. From it comes the sense of knowing, respecting and liking who you are. It helps you recognize your value and competence. It is your ultimate defense. It gives you the confidence to do what you want and need to do. It keeps the bad from beating you down. It eliminates any doubts you might have about your goodness, your value, your dignity, your right to a second, or even a third chance, and your right to be shown respect—even when you don't feel you deserve it.

Your core's invulnerability does not make you invulnerable to physical harm, but physical harm is the least of your concerns. Physical harm is usually the easiest thing to control. It is the emotional harm and its enduring impact that will beat you down. Even when you suffer from a terminal illness or a severe injury, the emotional impact can be the difference between maximizing your positive experiences and being engulfed by emotional devastation and hopelessness.

Your Core Protects You

The loss of a job, relationship, or health cannot breach your core. Embarrassment, disappointment, failure, and victimization cannot breach your core. You are free from external threats because your core protects you.

The point of this entire discussion is this: You are imperfect, you will make errors, you will have failures, and bad things will happen, but your core protects you from all of that. It is your shield. It keeps you free. Recognizing and understanding these facts allows you to risk being second best, losing, being labeled, not knowing, being rejected, and stumbling. You will not be hurt, and you will not be destroyed.

Further, your core allows you to recognize, with all of that, you still have value, you still have your core identity, and you still have the right to be. Finally, it gives you the ability to try again, to succeed and to grow. With this core, you know you will survive. You know you will heal. You know you will get back up and you know you have value. Your foundation cannot be hurt. You will learn from those experiences. You will learn from the past. You will look to the future. You will plan a new strategy. You will attack it with positive energy and strength. Finally, you will find your place.

The Key Is Engaging Your Core

So, why is it, then, you can hurt so badly if, indeed, you have this core? It is because your core is not engaged and therefore its shielding effect is not activated. If you do not engage your core's shielding effect, you spontaneously allow the input from people and events to break through, distract, disrupt and hurt you. But it's not the input from other people and events that destroys you. It is the fact that your core is not engaged that allows the bad to cause you so much pain. Your core is always there. It always has the power to shield. All you need to do is engage it. Like a boxer, while he always has his fists gloved and ready, he must engage them to shield blows from his opponent and to strategically attack. He does this by keeping his gloves raised— not simply in defensiveness, but as part of a winning strategy. You engage your core similarly—to protect you from those things that threaten you. You are strategically avoiding, coping with, responding to, adjusting, and beating them.

Your core not engaged   Your core engaged

You need to engage your core, especially during the most difficult times. Most people only engage their cores sometimes. During painful times, your core can become disengaged. You may feel particularly vulnerable, beaten, panicked, or empty. You might not be able to breathe. When it is difficult to engage your core, it is most precisely at these times, that it is especially important to make a conscious, concerted effort to engage it.

Engaging Your Core – The Difference It Makes

What is the difference between those who get past a terrible event and those who are beaten by it? Why do some people follow a road of perpetual despair or self-destruction while others do not? The primary difference is those who are able to refocus, pull themselves up, regroup and try again are those who have engaged their core. They have an inner sense of strength and security—even after experiencing devastating events. They are not threatened at the core level. They are able to separate what they did or what happened to them from their value and their identity. They don't obsess about what people will think, drown in the past, or expect a bleak future. They do not get mired in dread and doom and become reactive and self-destructive. Instead, they learn from the bad and jump to the next opportunity to succeed and grow. They don't get defensive. They get strategic. They don't get depressed. They get strong. They don't get paralyzed. They get mobilized. They don't dwell on the past. They reach for the future.

What Happens To Us When We Do NOT Engage Our Core

With our core disengaged, we become distracted, reactive to, and haunted by the negative events in our lives. We create negative scenarios for the future. We may go into an inward defensive mode becoming isolated, paralyzed, depressed, and quiet. We do whatever it takes to not get hurt again.

Or we may go into an outwardly defensive mode; attacking, lashing out, insulting, or resisting those who have hurt us. We may even do those things to people who have never, or would never hurt us. The sad thing is that our core is always in place regardless, but people who haven't engaged their cores typically don't know it. Therefore, they feel personally threatened (and that threat tends to be magnified) and they become emotionally and sometimes physically reactive.

So, it's like a woman who believes she is being followed. She becomes frightened and panics. She runs right past a police officer and into traffic, and she gets hit by a car and dies. Though there was an officer there to protect her, she wasn't aware of him, so she did not seek his help. She ran right past him and she was killed.

When your core is not engaged, you are prone to be pulled along a path of negativity, over-reactiveness and recurrent self-destruction, making one bad decision after another when things go bad. With your core engaged and your knowledge and understanding that each event is separate and has a start and an end, you can take control at any point in time. Then, identify and take a new path to a positive future.

Ultimately, you must engage your core in order to survive and flourish. You must get to know your core and feel its presence. This is not always an easy task, but it can be achieved if you are willing to trust in yourself and seek out your core. If you do not engage your core, you risk becoming preoccupied (perhaps subconsciously) with being hurt, previous injustices against you, or your own flaws. You can become reactive, defensive, paralyzed, avoidant, isolating, combative, self-destructive, bitter, reckless, angry, or depressed, and ultimately irreversibly damaged. Engaging your core keeps you focused on your future, on growth, opportunity and logical, positive, future-oriented response. It just lets you be yourself. It also keeps you from becoming overwhelmed with, and preoccupied by, past events and the thoughts and actions of people who might have purposefully or inadvertently hurt or devalued you.

I am not saying that you should not be concerned about negative events and outcomes. Nor am I saying that you should not take time to grieve when you face severe loss. I am saying that at some point you must approach them objectively and strategically. I am urging you to look at them from a position of strength and confidence—and not to attach them to your value or identity. Even when your emotions are understandably high, maintain a level of objective thought by engaging your core.

Your core is not some poetic abstraction. It is not a made-up thought to help you feel better. It's real. How can you be sure? You can be sure because you know that no one can decide that you are worth less than you were yesterday, therefore you are. Or, that you are worth less than John, therefore you are. In fact, your value is undeniable. No one can change that. Similarly, no one can say you're bad, guilty, stupid, inept, silly, or incompetent, or anything else, for that matter, and therefore you are. Look at it this way: If someone says you're a genius, does that make you one? Of course not. So why would it be possible with a negative statement? It's not. Your value and your identity are pure and undeniable. They are protected deep in your core. While people can say anything they want, they cannot change your value or dictate who you are. Your core is real.

Example: After she broke up with him, he dreaded going to the party. He knew everyone there would be checking him out and making assumptions about their relationship, and about him. He already felt beaten up and insecure by the breakup. They obviously would see him as incapable of keeping her interest. They would think he was not rich enough, good enough, handsome enough, or smart enough. Quite frankly, that was how he saw himself since the breakup. But, if he had engaged his core, he would have realized he was no different than he was before the breakup.

But since he hadn't, he felt devastated. The fact is that their perceptions of him would be based more on his behavioral response and emotional reaction to the situation than on the fact that she had left him. This is true in most all situations.

So where does all this leave you during tough times? It leaves you with having to engage your core and respond strategically to avoid the negative emotional impact of an event, and then reposition yourself from a position of strength. Future growth is your immediate objective after any negative event. You can destroy your reputation, standing, relationships, goals, options, and confidence by getting stuck in an event. Try to avoid pulling in, lashing out, obsessing on the past, beating yourself, or doing nothing. The way you respond and reposition yourself is critical. Engaging your core is essential. Engaging your core reinforces the foundation of your value and your identity. It provides you the protection from what people do, say, or feel about you. It protects you from any negative events that happen to you. It also provides the energy to focus, overcome, succeed, and grow.

But, what happens if you feel like you have no value? What happens if you feel like you are truly worthless? Consider this. If a friend told you he felt worthless because of something he did. Then he listed off the same things you have identified in your own life that support your contention that you have no value. Would you think your friend was correct and that he was worthless? Chances are you wouldn't believe he was worthless. Why are you of any lesser value than your friend.

If this exercise does not change your mind right away, let the concept simmer. Don't try to fight it or embrace it. Just let it sit there.

Even a mother who turns away from her child for just one brief moment and her child falls down the stairs and dies, as understandably devastating as that would be, can engage her core to get her eventually back to that solid foundation on which to begin to rebuild the rest of her life. While experiencing the undeniably excruciating devastation, she may not forgive herself or want to go on living, but she still can engage her core. It will help put her on a path to begin forgiving herself and stop beating herself up. To believe she has the right to go on living. Her core will recognize her deeper value and the fact that there is still a place for her. It will reassert that her core identity is not a person who let her child die. It will remind her that her identity is found much deeper.

With her core engaged, she will summon and focus her strength and go on living. When a person does something that is devastating, he/she has three options: 1) Stop living (literally, or figuratively). 2) Continue focusing on and experiencing, the devastation, or 3) Engage her core, which will bring about opportunities to go forward, refocus on the future, grow, and do good. Doing good is always the best strategy for getting past grievous errors, devastation, adversity, and hopelessness. Doing good gives us renewed focus, meaning, and strength. It's not about forgetting a past devastating occurrence, decision or action. We likely will never forget it. We don't have to. It's about moving forward.

In that kind of situation, grieving is necessary. Self-anger and despair are understandable. So, the possibility of this mother forgiving herself probably, in her mind, would not be an option. But as soon as she is able to engage her core, she will begin the process of healing.

Right about now, you might be asking, what is the value of a despicable person such as a child molester? Does this person have a core? And if so, does that mean he has value? Is that value the same value as other people? These are critical questions, and the answers can be easily misinterpreted. So, read the following sections very carefully:

People who do despicable things do have a core that is invulnerable to all things and all people, just like yours. The core makes their value undeniable and it houses their core identity, which is pure. The core lies beneath anything anyone has ever done. It gives people the solid foundation on which to rebuild their lives and do good—if they have the will to do so.

But let's be clear, here. Yes, their core, just like the cores of all people, house their value and identity that are protected, pure and undeniable. It also gives them a solid foundation to live, grow, lose, fail, and make mistakes—even horrible ones, and then get past them. But, their cores are not licenses for them to do terrible things for personal gain, at the expense of others.

A man who kidnaps, molests, or murders a young child still has a core. If engaged, it will tell him that he still has value and an identity that is deeper than the thing he did. It gives him the ability to change, grow, learn, and improve his life—even if he is in prison.

The core never justifies the negative act. It does not defend or excuse a purposefully abusive action. That is not its function. It's function is to give a person the power to grow from the act and improve without self-beating. It does not relieve a person from personal responsibility or regret. A man who mugs an elderly woman can engage his core, recognize his actions were wrong, pay the price (prison and/ or monetary restitution), take responsibility, forgive himself, accept himself, learn from the situation, grow from the situation, and move on to do better things. It does not suggest, in any way, that it was all right to mug the woman, or that it's okay to do it again, because "I can just engage my core again."

So, if you, indeed, did do something terrible, even despicable and purposeful, your engaged core can allow you to, in spite of your original intent, have regret and craft a strategic plan to change, grow, and give back in any way you can. Does it mean that what you did was not so bad? No, it was bad. But it means that you can (and should) move beyond it, focus on the future, do good, and grow. You will be freed from lifelong self-beating and self-hatred—even when others believe you should go on suffering—even for the rest of your life.

Is there a moral purpose for going on? Yes. If you don't, you can't do good going forward. But if you engage your core and go forward, you can help to repair the world and lessen other people's pain. That is the ultimate moral obligation. So, keep living. It is critically important.

Understand How Your Core Functions

The first step is thoroughly recognizing and understanding that your core is there. It exists. Do this by rereading these sections about your core several times until the lessons sink in. The second step is visualizing it. While you might not sense it yet, you still can visualize what it looks like. Initially, your core can be illusive. If you have not had a strong sense of your core for the majority of your life, it has likely been rendered dormant. It will have to be re-energized like the engine of a car that has not been driven for months. Like a cold neglected engine, it is not going to start up the minute you turn the key.

In the case of the car engine, while you may have never really examined one, you most likely have some general insights as to how it looks and what it does. You know it's heavy and metal, you put gas in the tank, you turn the key, and you step on the pedal to move the car. While the engine is the heart of a car and impacts every part of it, your core is the heart of you. It impacts every aspect of you. But, like the engine, the core needs to be approached, energized and coaxed into operation. They both need to be engaged.

Visualize your core as the very center of your heart. It has strands that extend in all directions. When not engaged and energized, they appear as thin white threads. They are devoid of all color—just like the core is devoid of all impact from all things. Just as you would coax your engine into running, you coax your core into running. When your core is engaged, the white strands glow. When your core's strands glow, they become silvery beams of energy. They produce light all around you. When they are energized, your core is engaged. When your core is engaged, it sends its energy throughout your brain and your body. When your core is engaged, you have strength, focus, identity, and awareness of your value. When your core is engaged, you are protected.

When you are in a threatening situation, visualize the threads of your core beginning to glow as beams of positive silvery energy. See them glow in your heart and in your brain. When tension rises, see the beams of silvery energy grow even brighter. See and feel the beams shooting up and down your arms and legs. They reach every finger and every toe. See and feel them running through your neck and your torso. See them running throughout every neuron in your brain. Every cell of your body has a silvery glowing beam pulsing through it. They are energizing, warming, revitalizing, repairing, and protecting. They reinforce and strengthen you in every way.

As you engage your core, recognize that your value and your identity are strong. You are invulnerable to all things and all people in the past, present, and future.

Just as the cold long-unused engine initially will hesitate and resist your efforts, this is also true of your dormant core. It will appear to resist. Similar to the engine, the more you take care of your core and the more frequently you run it, the better it will operate. The more you engage it, take care of it, and connect with it, the more willing and able it will be to be there for you when you need it. It will do what you need it to do.

Your core will provide you what you need in order to be strong, happy, and in control, but it does not solve all your problems. There will always be problems. But the core will give you the tools you need to deal with them most effectively, and to weather the bad times and get to the good ones. Wouldn't it be nice to not have any bad things happen? But, as we said, that is not possible. What is possible, however, is that there will be fewer bad things that happen to you, and that the bad things that do happen to you will no longer hurt you the way they have hurt you before, or are hurting you now. You will no longer be paralyzed, beaten down, or stripped of your energy, focus, and dignity. This is because your core will provide protection, awareness of your core identity, awareness of your undeniable value, and the strength to act, endure, and deal with bad things. You will do this strategically and effectively—from a position of strength and confidence—and you will grow.

Keep in mind, your core is not something that is foreign. It's nothing you have to create, or put into yourself. It's already there. You were born with it. You live with it. You will die with it. You simply need to engage it and turn those thin white threads into the glowing silvery beams of positive energy.

How do you know if your core is engaged? You will feel it. It will start as brief moments (maybe just a few seconds) of relief, warmth, hope, strength, and self-acceptance. Look for it. As you consciously attempt to engage your core during times of stress, it will soon begin to engage itself spontaneously. In time, your typical reaction to stress will be the spontaneous engagement of your core. You'll have strength and focus. You will feel valuable and confident as you move forward, plan, and grow.

Engaging Your Core

To engage your core, sit back, breathe fully but easily, close your eyes and visualize the thin white threads. Feel them becoming strong, glowing silvery beams of energy.

Visualize each part of your body beginning to glow. Start with your head, eyes, nose, mouth, ears, neck, and shoulders. Work your way down your body until every part of you is relaxed. If you don't feel it right away, repeat it until you do. Look for small initial signs and feelings. Feel as the beams of energy pulsate through every cell in your body.

Identify your core value. While you see and feel your core being engaged, strong and bright throughout your body, recognize that you have undeniable value that is not dependent upon what other people do, say, or think. It is not dependent upon what you do, say, or think (even if you aren't completely sold on this concept—yet).

Recognize your core identity. Your core identity and value are beneath your faults and flaws—and in spite of them. Strive to grow, improve, and to do good. (we all should), but realize that who you are is not dependent upon what you do or what other people do, say, or think.

Identify your core invulnerability. Your personhood and value—complete with dignity, wholeness, the right to exist, your right to second, third, or fourth chances, and your right to be happy. Recognize they cannot be stripped away by anyone or anything, (even if you aren't completely sold on this concept—yet). Say these statements out loud. Write them down so you continue to give yourself the same messages consistently.

Practice engaging your core. Practice the first steps every day—as many times as you can. Say the statements out loud and to yourself—while breathing normally and fully.

While the steps are simple, they can be challenging to wrap your mind around. But don't be daunted. The more you practice them, the easier they will become. With more practice, you will feel your core. Keep in mind, engaging your core is not an all-or-nothing proposition. Like turning on a faucet, it starts with a drip, then a trickle, then a stream, and then a rush. At first, you may only feel it for a moment at a time. If you feel it, recognize it, celebrate it, and nurture it. It will grow—and so will you.

When you feel devastated, engaging your core can feel close to impossible. You may even feel guilty about trying to engage your core if you feel responsible for something very bad. You might be saying, "What right do I have to feel better?" You do have the right ... and the obligation to feel better. because remember, only if your core is engaged, can you go on and do good for others. That is your obligation.

Tenet 6

Every human being, at the innermost level, has a core that houses and protects their identity and value that are free and invulnerable to all things and all people. Remember that, especially during difficult times. Know it's there. Think of it. Feel for it. Visualize it. Sense it. Talk to it. Taste it. Smell it. Embrace it. Practice engaging it—often.

Notes

PART 3

Finding Your Place in the World

So here you are, an imperfect human being who may be enduring heartache, anger, disappointment, fear, embarrassment, loss, frustration, failure, or alienation. But … you now know you are a human being who has this core that protects you and houses your undeniable value and core identity. You also now understand the limited strength of events—even the worst ones—so you are well on your way toward finding your place.

The next step to finding your place is to understand what your needs are. This is because it is your needs that motivate and steer you throughout your life, and it is how you meet those needs that either assists, or hampers your efforts to find your place.

Chapter 6

Understanding Your Needs

*E*verything you think, feel, do, and say are your attempts to meet specific needs. So, it is critical that you understand your needs and how they function in order to understand why you feel what you feel, think what you think, do what you do, and say what you say. This will also help you understand why others think what they think, feel what they feel, do what they do, and say what they say. Finally, it will also help you understand why events and people impact you the way they do.

Once you are able to do that, you will be well on your way to harnessing the energy and power of the negative people and events in your life that currently beat you down. Once the energy is understood and harnessed, the events and people become far less threatening, nebulous, frustrating, devastating, insulting, humiliating, uncontrollable, mysterious, confusing, frightening, and overwhelming.

Then you can much more effectively wrap your arms around each one of them, and control, adjust, avoid, cope with, and even use them to your advantage—even those that are most challenging. Once you are able to do that, you are freed from their grip. They will no longer suck you in, paralyze you, and beat you down. Instead, they will actually catapult you to a positive future. Then you will be able to find your place.

The Five Basic Needs

While we can all easily identify hundreds of things we need on any given day. Abraham Maslow, a twentieth-century psychologist, identified five basic levels of human need that he said every human being strives to fulfill. He called them the "hierarchy of needs."

Five Basic Levels Of Needs—Adapted From Maslow's Hierarchy Of Needs

Adapted from Maslow, Abraham H, Motivation and Personality, 2nd. ed., New York, Harper & Row, 1970

1.) *Survival.* This is your need for life-sustaining elements, including food, water, and protection from extremes that directly threaten your life.
2.) *Safety and security.* This is your need for physical safety, financial safety, spiritual safety, safe relationships, and safety from any real or perceived threat to you or anyone who is important to you.
3.) *Belonging/connectedness.* This is your need to connect to someone or something. It may be a person, but it could be a career, a cause, a belief, a philosophy, a spiritual entity, a goal, or a dream.
4.) *Positive self-concept.* This is your need to be perceived as valued, respected, significant, and relevant. The lack of this consideration is a common cause of reactivity, defensiveness, violence, despair, abuse, emotional devastation, destructiveness, and self-destructiveness.
5.) *Self-actualization.* This is your need for fulfillment and achievement, including the need to move beyond mediocrity.

Maslow suggested that everything we do is in some way, intended to meet one of these five basic levels of need. These needs make up the foundation of the human experience. Which need you are trying to meet at any given moment depends upon what is going on in your life at that moment. Maslow also suggested that in order to meet a particular level's need, the prior levels' needs must first be met at that moment. Though a need level may be met at one particular time, at another, it may not be.

Example: You may be starting to write your second novel—sitting at the self-actualizing level—at two o'clock in the afternoon. At two thirty, you get a letter from the publisher. Your first novel has been rejected. You might find yourself thrust back into the self-concept level of need as you experience the emotional pain of hearing that your work and your talent, in other words, you—weren't good enough.

Tenet 7

Every behavior, feeling, or desire is intended, ultimately, to meet a basic need or is a reaction to not meeting, or potentially not meeting, such a need. When, during, or after an event, you find yourself in distress, you have to realize that the distress comes, not from the event, itself, but from a basic need level related to the event that is not being met.

This is apt to be a difficult concept to wrap your mind around, but it is a very important distinction. This will become clear as we move on through this book.

Distress and Need

Distress of all kinds always comes from one or more of these basic levels of need not being met. Therefore, during any negative event, it is important to recognize that the distress following a particular event is not the result of the event itself. You recognize the event is only the trigger. Following several steps can help you recognize the difference.

First, identify which basic need is not being met and how the event is related to it. Once you have done that, you can deal with the negative event more strategically, effectively, and objectively. You will have more focus and control. You will feel less distress, emotion, reactivity, chaos, and most importantly, with less dependence on it. This is because you are dealing with your basic need, completely separate from the event. Therefore, the event is only an event—with a start and an end. It has no more significance than that. This leads to the second step which is to directly respond to that basic need without becoming entangled in the specifics of the event.

Consider this example: Your work team has been charged with designing a new product to clean carpets. One team member, John, accuses you of being far too inexperienced to be of any use to the team. He laughs off or criticizes every idea you bring to the table. By the end of the meeting, you are furious, frustrated, and humiliated.

This is the first event and the natural tendency is to immediately focus on the event (John and the things he said). If you engage your core to get past John and the event, you will be able to focus not on how he hurt your feelings, insulted you, or demeaned you, but instead, on your basic need underlying the event that is not being met. You will be able to respond objectively to the event without being emotionally sucked in, dependent on it, or beaten by it and then emotionally (either internally, or externally) reacting to what he said. Here, the basic need that is not being met is self-concept.

If you look at this situation from the perspective of meeting basic needs, your self-concept need was not fulfilled when John snubbed you, insulted you, and embarrassed you in front of your colleagues. In this case, you would not continue to focus on John, or on getting snubbed. In other words—the event, because your value is not reliant on the event, and because doing so would only frustrate you since John already made his comment and you will probably not be able to change his mind—certainly not by arguing with him, or demanding that he change his view.

You would, instead, engage your core and focus, on the need, itself. You would objectively explore your emotional reaction to having your self-concept need threatened. Look at your attempts to protect your value and dignity and your feelings of anger, humiliation, or doubt. Engage your core. With your core engaged, you will realize there is no real threat to you or your value. This will free you from what's already occurred, and it will get you focused on your future, your goals, and your growth. You can't change what's been. You can't change John. Don't try.

With your core engaged, you recognize that your value, in fact, is not at risk. It is not determined or threatened by John. In an unemotional manner, you sit back and explain to John in a non-defensive and an educative flavor, that his attitude is hurting the entire team.

You say, "My idea is valid, in spite of any drawbacks you identify. Let's discuss your concerns." Ask John to back up his flippant statements with fact. You do all this from a perspective of strength. Here, you're not dealing with John's attitudes, and you are not defending your value to John, yourself, or anyone else. You're moving to a new event from a position of strength—one where your value is not at stake, and you are not trying to defend, prove, or protect it.

Here, you met your self-concept needs, not by convincing John you were right, not by arguing, or lashing back, but by responding from a position of strength. Your self-concept was fed by your response, not depleted by John's actions and statements. Finally, your value was not, in any manner, determined by whether or not your idea was a good one, whether John liked it, or whether John would eventually like it.

Even if John continued to berate you or your ideas, or even if John did, indeed, back up his contention that your idea was wrong—even inept, you would already be beyond that. You would be beyond that because it was not your goal to prove your value to him or to anyone. Your goal would be to initiate a new event that was more objective and constructive. Then move on. Remember, your idea may, or may not have been right, smart, or good. Regardless, your value was not in the balance. Regardless, you'd come out on top because with your core engaged, your value is secured, and you therefore respond from a position of strength. If you are right, it will come out. If you are wrong, you are wrong. If so, acknowledge his point; "John, I get your point." Then, the event is in the past. It's done. Leave it alone and move on.

If you want to, you can say, "I realize, now, my idea would not work, but my goal was to come up with a new idea that would reduce the number of repairs on the machinery which is important and warrants discussion. Let's talk about that."

That way, you maintain some control without having your ideas or concerns completely discounted without consideration.

Tenet 8

During a conflict that questions your value, engage your core, and from a position of strength, attend to your basic need, not the specifics of the event. Then respond by creating a new event. Then move on to your future and your growth. Remember, never react to, draw out, or perpetuate, a negative event—create a new one.

So now you know you are always working on meeting your needs. In fact, everything you think, feel, do, or say is designed to meet your needs in some manner. But, in order to meet your needs most effectively and live a life with less pain, frustration and regret, you have to change the way you process the challenging events in your life. Because it is how you process that impacts how you will respond to the events in your life. You have three vehicles you can use to process, deal with, and respond to, the events in your life.

Notes

PART 4

Meeting Your Needs

As you strive to meet your needs, you may face adversities, derailments, disappointments, humiliations, frustrations, roadblocks, embarrassments, loneliness, or emptiness. What do you have at your disposal to help you survive them? You have thoughts and emotions, which are the first two vehicles that form and determine your response to the things that threaten your ability to meet your needs and find your place.

They are followed by the third vehicle, the behavior that you choose to meet your needs. It is the sole objective of every thought, emotion and their resulting behaviors, to see to it your basic needs are met.

Chapter 7

The Three Vehicles

ach of the three vehicles has a particular function.

- Thoughts analyze events and situations and their potential impacts as objectively as possible. They also consider your potential responses to them, and they analyze how those responses may impact your needs, others' needs, the event, or situation in general, and your life (now and in the future).
- Emotions motivate you. They provide the motivational energy for committing to your needs and to performing the activities required to meet your needs. Positive emotions motivate you by infusing positive anticipation and excitement in meeting a need. Negative emotions motivate you by infusing a sense of negativity, vulnerability, and urgency in reaction to a perceived threat to meeting a need. Emotions also release energy, which in moderation, will reduce pressure in a healthy, safe manner. If in excess, they can release pressure explosively, causing great damage.
- Behaviors get the deed done. They are your actual physical responses to situations needed to protect and meet your needs. They carry out the wishes generated by your thoughts and emotions.

Balancing Your Thoughts, Emotions, and Behaviors

Your emotions, thoughts and behaviors, each impact the other two, every waking second of your life. All three are necessary to effectively deal with, and respond to, your needs. But any one of the three, if not balanced by the other two, can cause great problems:

Take this example: You're walking down the street and get robbed at gunpoint.

- If you respond with thought, but without emotion or behavior, you are likely to initiate objective analysis and assess risk, but without the personal commitment, the energy and the action needed to, either protect yourself, to fight, or to flee.
- If you respond with emotion, but without thought or behavior, you are likely to release unbridled emotional energy (anger, fear, depression) and assume potentially exaggerated and/or inaccurate impact or significance without clear objective analysis to rein in your biases, inaccurate assumptions or rash judgments, and again, without doing anything about it. Without behavior, all this energy is bottled up inside causing extreme anxiety and internal struggle.
- If you respond with behavior, but without emotion or thought, you are apt to spontaneously, impulsively, and somewhat passively act (run a few steps or make a halfhearted effort to resist) but without clear objective analysis, focused energy, or commitment to maintaining your efforts and getting the job done.
- If you respond with emotion and behavior, but without thought, you might release unbridled emotion with reactive behavior where you explode with rage and try to fight the armed gunman, but without considering the risk. Or you might run in fear without considering that risk.

You need all three in balance in order to meet your needs. When faced with a challenging event, ask three questions before you act:

- Have I thought this through objectively and considered all the risks and pitfalls?
- Are my emotions driving my decision without consideration of the objective facts? Are they in line with the reality of what is going on?
- Are the behaviors I am selecting appropriate (legal, ethical, safe, responsive) to my needs and future goals?

A Closer Look at Emotion

Emotion warrants a closer look since it gives your thoughts the motivation and energy necessary to act. It is also the emotional element that tortures us when things happen in our lives that scare, embarrass, disappoint, hurt, frustrate, or anger us. Emotional processing is much stronger than objective processing or passive behavior.

Simply thinking about something, or doing something, does not make it happen. You must be motivated through emotion to act, and your behavior must be energized to complete the task. In many cases, the emotion is minimally noticeable. At its lowest level, it is nothing more than a tug on you to get something done, but it's there. Midlevel emotions bring healthy desire or ambivalence. Higher-level emotions bring strong feelings, urges, and positive or negative drives. The highest-level emotions bring excessiveness, obsessiveness, panic, rage, despair, fanaticism, or euphoria.

Further, thinking about something that happened or might happen in the future does not bring with it the worry, anger, frustration, dread, aggravation, or fear, all of which have the power to torture you if they are not dealt with quickly. It is emotion, at its higher and highest levels (negative, in these cases), that you infuse into an event that can take you down a long, miserable road.

When Emotion Becomes a Problem

Your negative emotions can become a problem if they become unbalanced. This is when the emotion is outweighing objective thought and appropriately responsive behavior. When this occurs, you only experience the negative without any vision of the good, and you are feeling the negative energy with little, or no objective thought. This may result in lashing out or self-beating. Negative emotions are a particular problem when they are unchecked and allowed to gain momentum. They bring rash reactions to perceived threats to your value and safety (or the safety of a loved one).

Positive emotions can also be problematic. If they are unbalanced, you are going to experience the good and the excitement, perhaps rising to the level of euphoria, without being anchored which helps in considering the risks or potential negative impact.

It will serve you well when you are in the midst of a challenging event, to evaluate your use of the three vehicles (emotion, thought, and behavior) to determine if any are being underutilized or overutilized. This will reduce the negative impact of not thinking things through, overreacting, underreacting, or misinterpreting the impact and significance of an event, which in turn, leads to negative, inappropriate, dangerous, or misdirected reactions and negative consequences.

Tenet 9

Your thoughts, emotions, and resulting behaviors are the three vehicles used to meet your needs. Your thoughts impact your emotions and your behaviors, your emotions impact your thoughts and behaviors, and your behaviors impact your emotions and your thoughts. When you are faced with emotional pain, be aware of all three—their roles, their intensity, and how each is being used during and after any given event. Be sure to keep them in balance. Remember, when it is time to select a strategy to resolve

an internal or external conflict, it is critical that you consciously temporarily separate yourself from your emotions.

Triggered Emotions

When it comes down to it, your emotions are reactions to (triggered by) four occurrences. When you feel emotions overcoming you, it's critical to determine which one you are dealing with.

- Value-triggered emotions respond to real or perceived threats to your value, significance, and relevance. They result in defeatism, defensiveness, rashness, anger, or vengeance.
- Goal-triggered emotions respond to real or perceived threats to your goals and priorities, resulting in strategizing and responsiveness.
- Loss-triggered emotions respond to loss, or potential loss, of someone or something dear to you, resulting in sorrow, loneliness or emptiness.
- Achievement-triggered emotions respond when you receive validation of your value, significance, relevance, or achievement of goals. They result in celebration, relief, and security.

Consider this example of three people who go in for a theater audition. The first two fail to land parts. One falls apart and threatens to give up the theater entirely. He isolates and mopes. He states he knew he wasn't any good, and this proved it. Finally, he asserts the whole acting field is bogus.

The second person sets her sights on the next audition. She is driven to objectively evaluate her audition. She identifies a few ways she can improve and then focuses on the future (her next audition).

The third person gets the part. She is excited, calls friends, and celebrates.

The first one (incorrectly) connected his value to how well he did, and value triggered emotions set in. The result was defensiveness and defeatism. The second did not connect this event to her value—and it wasn't. She identified a threat to a key goal of hers, so goal-triggered emotions set in and motivated her to objectively and strategically prepare for the next event when she will, again, attempt to reach her goal. When the third person got the part, achievement-triggered emotions set in. She celebrated her achievement.

Tenet 10

If you experience negative emotions, determine if you're feeling a value or loss-triggered emotion. If it is, then engage your core. That will de-energize the emotion and detach your value, your sense of loss and your decisions from the event and those emotions. You'll be left with the motivating goal-triggered emotions that are needed to move forward.

What Triggers Emotion

Events do not come with their own specific, assigned, or inevitable emotions. Emotions are generated solely within each of us. You subconsciously apply a specific interpretation, meaning, and significance to a given event. The specific emotion is triggered by this interpretation. You assign a level of importance to the event, depending upon your view of yourself, your past experiences, your perceptions, and your assumptions surrounding it.

This fact is important because it tells you your emotions are not slaves to events. It tells you, you can adjust your emotions and the impact of them. Not by simply saying "I'm not going to let that make me mad." Few people have that kind of control. You do it by engaging your core. Doing so defuses and detaches the event at hand from the tight grip of your emotion, and from any indication of, or relationship to, your value. This de-energizes, both the emotion and the event. Then, you are freed from the clenched grip of both of them, and you can approach the event, strategically, from a position of strength and objectivity.

Consider this example: John got beat again. Golf! He played with Fred every week. Every week, Fred walloped him and, boy, did he gloat. Then, of course, he bragged about it at the office, to everyone. John was embarrassed and angry. This continual ribbing always chewed John up until he was able to engage his core and separate the events of Fred beating him in golf and then ribbing him later on, from any specific emotion (and his value).

With effort and focus, John engaged his core and reminded himself (stating to himself repeatedly and then internalizing it) of the fact that being beaten in golf and the ribbing were two events that did not impact his value and were not cemented to any emotion. In other words, these two events were simply events. PERIOD.

Once he disconnected the emotion and his value from those two events, he was able to respond objectively instead of emotionally or reactively. What he did was this: When Fred would gloat, he just smiled slightly at Fred, then walked away. If Fred bragged to others, John would simply smile back, shaking his head slowly, just a touch, saying, "Yeah, he's good." He also stopped playing. Not because he was angry, or embarrassed, or to punish Fred—but simply because he didn't want to.

When John stopped connecting the two events to his emotions and his value, he found control by not playing golf with Fred and not reacting to him. Once he took control, he was no longer hurt. Fred ultimately stopped gloating.

Tenet 11

Don't act until you ask: "Why am I feeling this way and what need is being threatened?" Take the time to determine where your emotion is coming from and why? Consider the balance (or lack of balance) of thought, emotion and behavior, and identify how you use all three of them. Disconnect your emotion and value

from the event by engaging your core. Then respond strategically and objectively.

The Internal Energy of Emotions

Beware, a critical characteristic of emotion is that it has an internal energy that automatically gains momentum if left unchecked. Negative emotions tend to gain momentum that results in additional, or an intensifying of, those negative emotions, which further reduces objectivity and increases reactivity. Similarly, positive emotions bring additional positive energy. The point, here, is that during high emotional times, you have to recognize the tendency of the energy to sweep you up and carry you farther than you originally anticipated or wanted. Consider crimes of passion. Seldom are they planned—at least not objectively and intellectually. This tendency to be swept up occurs with positive as well as negative emotions.

Emotions, both positive and negative, seem to have lives of their own. So, if you are not vigilant, you can find yourself victimized by them, especially when you assume that the energy is uncontrollable and unavoidably attached to an event itself. Many people say, "I couldn't help myself." That is when the greatest damage is done.

It is easy to be surprised by this momentum instead of anticipating it, dealing with it, controlling it, or preempting it. The emotion and its energy seem to have the ability to self-justify, meaning you may just assume you are justified in, or simply have no control over, your anger, fear, defeatism, or helplessness (or euphoria, in the case of unbridled positive emotion), as well as whatever behavior you apply to it. Therefore, you keep it going—unchecked. So, looking back, you might say: "I was sick of people thinking I was incompetent. How else should I have felt? So I finally showed them. I yelled at all of them. What else could I have done? I had no choice. Besides, they deserved it." Unchecked, your emotions expand and deepen. Unchecked, your emotions can fester and overwhelm you. Unchecked, your emotions can result in severe damage to others and to yourself.

Tenet 12

When you're emotional—either positively, or negatively—recognize the energy and momentum. No decisions should be made until the energy ebbs and the momentum stops, or at least slows. Engaging your core gives you back control and stops, or slows the momentum.

NOTE: Remember, during your most challenging, painful times, if you are aware of, and you understand, your needs and the three vehicles you use to meet them, you will much more effectively meet those needs, with far less distress, and you will much more easily find your place.

Notes

Chapter 8

OCEANS Assessment

*D*uring particularly negative events, thoughts, emotions, and behaviors can intensify and run together—blurring facts and assumptions; insults and constructive criticisms; wants and needs. It can be difficult to tell the difference between right and wrong, good and bad, responsiveness and reactivity, and negative and positive visions of your future. You can easily become emotionally and physically victimized by these events, as the blurring seems to intensify and self-perpetuate, and the events suck you up like a tornado sucks up a small toy and tosses it hundreds of yards away—crumpled and broken. To deal with negative events that elicit strong negative emotions that inevitably hurt you, you need to break the self-perpetuating cycles of event-emotion-reactive behavior.

You can break this cycle by doing an OCEANS (Observations, Cognitions, Emotions, Assumptions, Needs, Strategies) assessment, whereby during, or after an event, you first, identify and separate your observations, cognitions (thoughts), emotions, assumptions and needs. Then look carefully at each one and select the best strategy to meet your needs. Take the time to separate them. This will slow down and weaken the self-perpetuating cycle of event-emotion-reactive behavior. It also will clarify each aspect of the event at hand so you can determine your best strategy for overcoming its challenges.

OCEANS Assessment Steps

First, identify what you observed during the event—only what you actually saw, first hand. "This is what I saw." Apply no meaning, emotion, or assumptions to it—and make no decisions based on it.

Second, identify your objective thoughts (cognitions). Determining what you know is true will help you objectively assess the situation in controlled fashion, and determine cause, mitigating circumstances, and potential results backed by logic and fact. Objectively consider the risks involved without emotion. Only absolute and/or logical certainties are included in this category.

Third, identify your emotions. How are you feeling? Be completely honest. By doing so, you immediately define them, which reduces their energy so you can think more clearly and act more strategically. Emotional processing is more reactive, spontaneous, and energized than objective thought. Unlike cognition, it is based on instincts, biases, and your sense of your own value, significance, safety (yours, or that of someone you care for) and wholeness, any of which can be highly distorted during negative events. So recognize what emotion is in play and where the emotion is coming from. Reducing its energy is critical. If you are experiencing more than one emotion, select the emotion you want to deal with first—perhaps the emotion that is most painful, disruptive or that puts you at greatest risk.

Fourth, identify your assumptions. What do you assume but not know for sure? This gives you a clear idea of what you know is true versus what you think is true. Explore the things you think are true, but be careful when acting on those assumptions. Do the same with what you think might happen versus what you know will happen.

It is during this fourth step that it is critical that you identify your assumption about how the event will impact your life. Ask questions. "How is this apt to impact me financially or emotionally? How will this impact my relationships, my job, my safety, or my reputation?"

Fifth, identify the impacted basic needs. Focus on the basic need impacted by this event and not the event itself. "Because of this event, I feel unsafe. (safety need); Because of this event, I feel valueless. Because of this event, my value is being doubted. (self-concept need); Because of this event, I feel alone. (belonging need)."

Sixth, select your strategy. Take into consideration your observations, thoughts, emotions, assumptions, and needs. Identify your goal and strategy for meeting the need you identified. Consider any risks, make your plan, and then take action. Focus on your future actions: "In order to _____, I will _____." Come up with several options and pick the best one.

Consider this example: You realize your wallet is gone and you know that someone picked your pocket. You are furious because you were violated and had seven hundred dollars in your wallet. You're anxious because you had credit cards in it, and you're sad because you carried a photo of your child in it, and you have no copy of it. You think you know it happened at the restaurant you just left. You stomp back to the restaurant and point your finger at the guy who you think took it. He denies it. You belt him and you get arrested. The problem, here, is that these events, emotions, thoughts and behaviors blurred into one uncontrolled force and resulted in one rash event. The problem, also, was that you clocked … the … wrong … guy … and … you … went … to … jail!

Using an OCEANS Assessment

Let's take a step back. After being pick-pocketed, if you had performed an OCEANS assessment, things might have turned out differently. In this case, you might have identified your:

… Observations (what you saw): "My pocket is empty and my wallet is gone."
… Cognition - objective thoughts (what you know to be true): "My wallet is gone. The last place I saw it was at the restaurant."
… Emotion (what you are feeling): "I am angry, anxious, frustrated, nervous, sad, and violated. Which emotion do I need to deal with first? I will deal with my nervousness knowing someone has my credit cards."

... Assumption (what you believe to be true): "The guy who knocked into me by accident must have stolen my wallet."

... Need (which of your need levels is at risk): Safety – "My financial safety is at risk. I lost a lot of money and my credit cards." Self-concept – "I'm feeling violated and weak because the guy was able to get my wallet. Belonging – "I lost something special between my child and me. Which need do I want to deal with first?

... Strategy (what you should do after considering the risks, if a current event): "I should contact the police to question the guy." "I should cancel my credit cards."

...strategies regarding future situations (what you will do next time if this kind of thing happens again), "I'll call the police or I will avoid the situation all together by putting my wallet in my front pocket."

...strategies regarding a past situation (what you might have done), "I might have called the police." "I might have checked the lost and found."

The OCEANS assessment allows you to see exactly what might happen or did happen and how you will or did respond. It also helps you let go of a negative event, once and for all. This is because the processing you do during an OCEANS assessment defuses the emotional energy surrounding the event, which lessens its grip on you, and engaging your core allows you to get through the event, let it go, and focus on the future.

Here is another example: Do you remember when you were a very young kid going through a haunted house for the first few times and how scary it was? It was scary because you didn't know how they created the scary things, and you were not able to determine when, or where the next scare would be coming. You also didn't know for sure what was and wasn't real, and you weren't sure you weren't at risk. Today you observe clearly what's in the house. You objectively understand the concept and intent of a haunted house. You know the ghouls are just people in costume. Your emotions, while perhaps kicked-in due to the exhilaration of the event, are in check. This is because while you may be surprised by a costumed ghoul jumping out at you, you are not fearing for your life. You assume you will be all right. You expect scary things to be coming up ahead, but they will not hurt you. Because you know it's just play and you are not at risk, your safety need level is not threatened or activated. You just keep walking forward. You expect surprises, but you do not overreact to what is going on. Here, you subconsciously and spontaneously, just did an OCEANS assessment.

You can also do an OCEANS assessment on a long-past situation or a decision that is haunting you, as long as your goal is to sort out and learn from the past, and then focus on the future in order to grow. Do not do so to ruminate on the past.

The next tenet is an important one, especially when you feel like making things better is impossible and that you are a victim of your thoughts or emotions, "I can't help the way I feel."

Tenet 13

Perform an OCEANS assessment. Separate the observations, cognitions, emotions, assumptions, and needs. Be sure to identify the basis of the emotion and the basic needs at risk. (Threats to your significance, value and relevance that have risen to the safety level are often at the root, and can be particularly challenging). Engage your core, and focus less on the event and more on your needs, your future and your larger goals, then set your strategy.

Can an OCEANS assessment work for a convicted murderer who is spending the rest of his life in prison? Yes. Even in that case, the murderer spending life in prison can assess his situation and strategize a response. He can't change the original event—murdering his victim and being incarcerated—but he can consider their impact on his life from now on, then strategize and institute a plan to change his perspective, identify his options, even if limited in number, and make his next positive moves toward making the most of the rest of his life in prison, instead of focusing on what he did and the freedom that he lost.

Now that you understand the events that occur in your life; key aspects of your nature; your needs; the vehicles available to you; and how you can assess, deal with, and respond to those things that threaten your needs, let's look at the specific barriers that get in your way of finding your place.

Notes

PART 5

What Keeps You From Finding Your Place

So, what is it that gets in the way of you finding your place? What is it that has the power to create so much self-consciousness, pain, chaos, uncertainty, frustration, sadness, insecurity, and anger in your life? What is it that can lead you to make bad decisions that ultimately hurt you or those you care about? Actually, as we discussed earlier, it has little to do with the challenging events that life throws at you. It has everything to do with how you interpret, react to, and respond to those events. To understand it all, it's critical to realize that at the very heart of this issue is how much you engage your core.

But, it is important to realize that a vicious cycle can easily be created. If you don't engage your core, it will negatively impact your ability to effectively interpret and respond to the events in your life; and your inability to interpret and respond to the events in your life will negatively impact your ability to engage your core. In order to break that cycle, you have to attend to both.

We already talked about your core and how to engage it. Now you need to address the Twenty-eight key barriers to objectively interpreting and effectively responding to the events that can reduce your power to engage your core, resulting in your experiencing pain, and not finding your place in the world:

What follows are the twenty-eight key barriers to finding your place in the world and what you can do about them.

Chapter 9

Allowing Events to Victimize You

(1)

*W*hen times are hard, when bad things keep happening, particularly when you are feeling insecure, overwhelmed, or self-conscious, or you suffer a loss, you may feel like you are at the mercy of the events that are happening to you. Even the anticipation of a potential, negative event can bring about dread, frustration, and panic. In those cases, you can feel victimized—even before anything happens. The problem is that, in these cases, you become emotionally dependent on events you believe you cannot control (if you could easily and immediately control them, there would be no problem—right?)

Since you believe you can't control the events (and maybe you can't), you become more and more insecure, anxious, frightened, frustrated, disillusioned, hopeless, panicked, or angry. This can often be followed by rash, reckless, or defensive decisions that result in rash, reckless, or defensive behaviors. Or, it can result in inaction, emotional paralysis, fatigue, ambivalence, or despair. Those are all signs of being victimized.

In these cases, you must look inside yourself, starting with your core. Why? Because it is at your core where you can be sure that you are independent, where you are in control, where you are safe, where you can go to regroup, where you can regain objectivity, where you can make change happen, and where you can begin to move on. In some cases, it may be the only place where you can make change happen. Keep in mind, turning to an inward focus is not the same as isolating yourself from the world, caving in to others' unjust actions or demands, or beating, or blaming yourself. It is about looking at the source of all control and change. It's about strategizing absolutely objectively—and that starts with you, and it starts in your core.

Consider this example: A woman lost her home in a fire. She lost everything. She was understandably in despair and enraged. Thankfully, her kids got out. She blamed her husband for leaving on the space heater that caused the fire. She blamed the builders of her house for using flammable materials. She blamed God for letting it happen, and she blamed herself. She felt completely out of control. The reality was that she could not change what happened, and she could not cope with the explosiveness inside of her that was just beneath the surface.

What she could do, however, is engage her core, then focus less on the events, whose fault it was and what happened (the external), and instead focus on her basic needs and what she would do now (the internal). No easy task. But by looking inside and doing something now that looks to the future, she could empower herself. She could break free of the binds of the past—even the immediate traumatic past—the external event. This doesn't mean to forget the past. It just means to look beyond it. To focus, in this case, perhaps on her safety needs (physical, financial and emotional) and work on creating a safer, more secure environment for her family and herself. Finally, her belonging needs—ensuring that her kids are coping with the trauma they just endured by helping them feel a very close connection with her.

Tenet 14

When things are not going well, focus inwardly. That is where you have control. Focus on your future. Don't focus on trying to change events that have already occurred, or on aspects of currently occurring events you can't change. Engage your core. Identify your basic needs at play, look to the future, and focus on what you can do now. There is always something you can do.

Notes

Chapter 10

Giving Events Absolute Significance

(2)

*W*e spoke of life being made up of many individual events with definite starts and ends, and your ability to start a new one at any time. Yet, you can so easily be victimized and paralyzed by an event that happens to you—even long after the event has ended.

When you perceive that the impact of an event is greater than its specific practical impact based on objective logic and fact; if you are sure its impact is unchangeable, unilateral (that it can mean only one thing), and that it defines you as good or bad; right or wrong; useful or not—then you're assigning absolute significance to the event and you're letting the event define your value absolutely. Then you are basing your value on assumptions, on exaggerated actual or potential impact, on emotions, and often based on absolutely worse-case scenarios.

By attributing absolute significance to an event, you victimize or paralyze yourself because absolute significance, by definition, is one-sided and cannot be changed. It's absolute, and if the event's absolute significance is negative, you have already lost. Long days of despair, loneliness, emptiness, humiliation, bitterness, fatigue, anger, fear, anxiety, depression, hopelessness, and self-consciousness result from an event attributed with absolute significance when you believe the event has absolute power to judge you and that there is no way to change the event's meaning or impact. This can leave you with the assumption that you are doomed.

The reality is that events have no absolute significance. They do have real objective impact. The difference is important to note:

- Real objective impact: "If I don't pass this test, I'll fail the class."
- Absolute significance: "If I don't pass this test, I'll fail the class. I'll never get into college. That will prove I'm stupid and a failure."

The Significance and Value of Events

As we just discussed, events have no absolute significance. The only significance they have is what you artificially apply to them. Therefore, anything that happens in your life is only as significant as you allow it to be. The point, here, is since the significance of an event is not absolute, while you may not be able to change the event, and it may have some impact on you, or even great impact on you, you can change your perspective, your interpretation, your participation, and your response to it. That can change your future in a positive way. Further, if you do not attribute absolute significance, or a great deal of artificial significance to an event, the event, then, has limited power and therefore can only cause you limited emotional pain. Finally, if you do not attribute absolute significance to an event, it cannot threaten your value, because the event is just an event, period!

So, how do you know that an event has no absolute significance? You know this because different people attribute different meanings, perspectives, and levels of significance to similar events—or even to the exact same event. Let me illustrate:

Four people get laid off from the same company, at the same

time, from the same position for the same reason—cut-backs. One person is devastated and depressed, another is angry, another could not care less, and another is relieved. The fact is, that these four different people had four different reactions to the identical event. This was due to the different significance they attributed to it. This tells you that significance is determined by the individual, not defined by the event, itself.

Here is another example: You're out at the park watching a baseball game. The red team wins, the blue team loses. Some spectators are happy and some are sad. People driving by have no feeling about it, whatsoever. The event, itself, has no absolute significance. The meaning comes only as a result of a particular person's perspective, experiences, interpretation and his/her individual priorities.

Let's look at one more example: The ending of three romantic relationships. One person goes into despair, the other is relieved and the third is angry. The first one who is in despair, feels he has lost a part of himself and he assumes he will never find another like her. The second one who is relieved, feels he is now free and that he now can do things he wants to do—perhaps find someone better. The relationship to him was a hindrance. The third, who is angry, feels that he was wronged by the break up. He feels he was disrespected and violated.

The fact is that the same event carried with it three different levels and kinds of significance for three different people. This is very important and, in fact, very liberating for you because it tells you that you are not a slave to the events in your life, and to some pre-determined and arbitrary significance that automatically and irreversibly judges you as stupid, inept, bad, doomed, valueless, lost, etc.

The significance is different because people are different. Every person is working on his or her own needs in his or her own ways. Further, even if different people are working on the same need, they may be working on it in different ways, using different methods and coming from different perspectives.

So, you must consciously recognize that an event is just an event. It carries with it no absolute significance. Significance is artificial. You must say it. Remember, particularly while you are in the midst of a negative event and the period just following it, it is most difficult to get in touch with this concept. But it is precisely at these moments that it is most important that you do just that.

Remember, all emotional pain and reactiveness comes, not from any specific event, but from the interpretations, assumptions and significance you apply to it, and the beliefs you wrap around it. Therefore, it is useless to analyze, dissect, defend, or curse the event in order to change it, deny it, justify it, or condemn it. Why, because the event already happened—you can't change it and, because it holds no absolute significance, so you don't need to ruminate on it. Instead, look forward.

In all these examples, the answer for them is to engage their cores, focus on what they will do now, and focus on their future and on their growth.

You might be asking; "How can you say that an event has no absolute significance? How about the birth of a child? Is there no significance there?" My answer is, yes, of course, but the key point is that, even in this case, the significance is not universal, or absolute. The significance is only that, which anyone of us applies to it. While it might be disturbing, even morally reprehensible, to hear someone say the birth of a baby means nothing, the fact is that, practically speaking, for any particular person, it may mean just that—nothing. Spiritually, morally and cosmically, there may be an argument that there is a universality to this event and regardless of what any individual says, or feels about it, there still is significance. But, for any given person, a birth taking place on the other side of the country, (or even next door), may have little practical significance and will likely not impact his/her life. Would I be sad if I heard that a birth was unsuccessful? Of course, but not everyone would necessarily feel that same way. The significance is only that artificial one that each person applies to it.

Let's take this to one more level: How can we say that an event is just an event, without intrinsic meaning or value? How can we say the death of a loved one is not meaningful? I am not saying someone dying is not horrible, painful, devastating, or scary. I am saying that even this terrible event does not dictate a specific emotional, mental or physical response. It also does not dictate the fate of those who mourn the loss since the event is still an event, without absolute significance, or power. You still have freedom to determine your response—and your future.

Tenet 15

Since events have no absolute significance or power, they cannot determine your absolute value or fate. They also don't dictate your response. Therefore, when dealing with a negative event, never focus on the event itself, or on some values-laden judgment, or assumptions resulting from it. Doing so only deepens your distress. The event happened. It's done—Period! Instead, focus on what you will do now. Focus on your future and on your growth.

The Real Implications of Events

How can an event have no significance when it's obvious an event can, indeed, disrupt your life? What about the death of a spouse, the loss of a job, or flunking out of school? You might even ask, if events have no significance, and life is made up of events, then does life, itself, have no significance?

I am not saying that events have no impact. Events most certainly can impact you, severely in some cases. Events can impact your job, relationships, goals, and dreams. However, there is a difference between absolute significance, on the one hand, and impact (physical, or emotional), on the other. But even an event's impact is not absolute. You can always adjust some aspects of an event's impact on you— either short-term and/or long-term. Absolute significance connotes one and only one meaning; absolute judgment of value; and absolute determination of fate.

Value/fate-laden statements come from applying absolute (albeit inaccurate) significance to events, such as...

- "I broke my leg and can't play in the Olympics. I am such a loser."
- "If she leaves me, it proves I am worthless. I'll never find another."

While there can be no argument that an event may indeed have impact, unlike absolute significance statements, impact statements state logical and objective outcomes and observations based on facts. Events do not assert value, one singular meaning, or absolute or enduring outcome or fate. They state only logical and practical potential impact such as...

- "If I break my leg, I will not be able to play in the Olympics this year, and it may not be 100 percent better in time for the next one."
- "If she leaves me, I will be sad. I will feel alone, and I will feel insecure."

If you stick to the impact statements, you can strategically plan your next move. If you incorrectly apply absolute significance to these events, you may leave yourself with few (or no) options, as well as self-doubt, lack of vision of how to make things better, and a feeling of valuelessness leading to inevitable pain, paralysis, feelings of failure and self-perceived vulnerability—a victim.

Impact versus Absolute Significance Statements

- Impact statements are objective, rational, constructive, fair, and nonjudgmental.
- Absolute significance statements are subjective, emotional, destructive, biased, broad, and judgmental.

- Impact statements indicate initial emotional and (possibly ongoing) physical impact.
- Absolute significance statements dictate inevitable value and enduring ultimate fate.

- Impact statements are starting points.
- Absolute significance statements are ending points.

- Impact statements are useful.
- Absolute significance statements are useless.

Tenet 16

Differentiate between absolute significance statements and impact statements. Absolute significance statements commit you to an unchangeable status—no hope. Impact statements only identify a specific immediate result of an event that does not, by definition, predict broader implications. Deny the absolute significant statements. Use the impact statements, but only as your starting points for strategizing and taking action. An event's impact is not absolute.

Where Your Focus Should Be

When you are negatively impacted by a negative event, your tendency naturally is to focus on that event. But when you do that, you actually are re-emphasizing and reinforcing the very event you are trying to get past. You are also, in fact, trying to change (or wishing you could change) something (the event) that has already occurred. This is the opposite of what you want and need, because in the end, you can't change an event that has already taken place. In these cases, you need to focus, not on the event, itself. Instead, start with where you are right now—wherever the event has left you (its impact), Then focus on your future, on your goals, on what you will do next, and on your personal growth.

The question is, what do you need to do next to improve yourself, your position, how you feel, your outcome, your status, or your situation? (not how do you change the event, how do you deny it, how do you defend it, or explain it to others, or to yourself). Even in business, if you make an error, you can either focus on the error (the event) by regurgitating what took place; explaining, justifying, or defending what took place; or by worrying about the "inevitable" fallout from what took place. Or, you can focus on your future, and the future of your business, starting with where you are right now—wherever the event has left you.

There is a very important distinction between focusing on the event and focusing on the future and growth. Focusing on the event is narrow and defensive, and it sucks energy. Focusing on the future and on growth quickly takes you beyond the event. It is based on strength and strategy. It considers broad areas of possibilities, and it infuses energy.

Example: An angry customer will no longer do business with you because he received poor service. You stand to lose thousands of dollars a year. You have two choices.

- Focus on the event. Call the customer back, reduce your price, defend, apologize, beg, stew, worry, or focus on the event. Or …
- Focus on the future.

Focusing on the event usually stops with the event. It's shortsighted and similar problems tend to arise again. It lacks a vision for the future. Further, if it is hard to fix the event effectively, it is easy to become disillusioned, stuck, burned out, or bitter.

Follow these steps:

- Reduce the immediate damage if possible (call the customer).
- Shore up your system (change your procedures).
- Focus on the future (identify new goals, directions, processes, customers, or players)
- Be less dependent on a single customer.

While, with the growth focus, you may still start with the event to minimize immediate damage, you immediately begin to shift your focus to the future.

NOTE: Focusing on the event usually stops with the event, and it's short-sighted, so similar problems tend to arise again and again. It also lacks a vision for the future, so if it proves to be very hard to fix the event effectively, it is easy to become disillusioned, stuck, burned out, or bitter.

You should look at the event only to define what happened and why, and to identify a starting point for your next efforts toward your future and your growth—where you want to be and what you need to do to get there.

Consider this illustration: You aspire to be a professional singer. You practice and feel like you are doing your best but after you perform, the audience's response is lukewarm. You walk off the stage feeling devastated, embarrassed and feeling everyone is asking (how you could have ever thought you could sing. At this point you might give this event absolute significance and determine that you are talentless and inept; and that you were stupid to even think you could be a performer. So your dreams are crushed and you know it is the end. In fact, now is the time to step back, consider only the impact statements and carefully assess and strategize your next moves. Do an OCEANS assessment.

- What did I observe? The audience barely clapped.
- What do I know to be true? The audience did not show that they really liked my performance.
- How am I feeling? I feel deflated, depressed, and embarrassed.
- What are my assumptions? They felt I was not very good. I'm not good.
- What need is going unmet? My self-concept need.
- What is my strategy for the future? I am going to find someone who can give me objective feedback so I know whether I am good or not. Then, depending on the input, I'll either practice

to improve, find another audience for my work, or look for another line of work.

In this case, focus was only briefly on the event, but then immediately shifted to the future.

Tenet 17

When faced with an event that has substantial negative impact, do not focus on the event. Do not apply absolute significance to it because there is none. Focus on its impact, but, only as a starting point for assessing the situation and strategizing your next steps toward your future and your growth. Remember that impact is not absolute either.

Notes

Chapter 11

Decisions Based on Inaccurate, Limited and Distorted Information

(3)

*E*veryone makes hundreds of decisions every day. Some are easy and some are difficult. Some are highly significant, and some hardly noticeable. We all make decisions based on our observations, knowledge, emotions, assumptions, input from others, our needs, and how we process.

But, sometimes the decisions you make (as is the case with all of us) are based on inaccurate, limited, or distorted information. Some decisions are based on shortsighted perspective. The result is that, in these cases, you risk making decisions that cause damage to you, your goals, or others. What is lacking in these cases is a focus on concrete observations, facts, logic, and careful consideration of emotional influences or carefully vetted assumptions. Like in the following example:

On payday, your check is reduced by 15 percent. You assume that your pay was docked because last week your boss told you he was unhappy with a key decision you made. You burst into his office and resign. You give your boss a large piece of your mind. What you didn't know was that there was a temporary computer glitch that incorrectly cut everyone's paycheck by 15 percent. You apparently missed the memo. Damage done.

Tenet 18

Remember, it's never the event that determines your response. It's the thoughts, emotions, interpretations, meaning, assumptions, and needs that you wrap around that event. Make sure your information is complete, accurate, and based upon fact; that your emotions, behaviors and thoughts are balanced and carefully considered; and that your emotions are in check before you make a major decision. Do an OCEANS assessment to sort it all out. This ensures that you are clear about the entire event. Of the things you still remain unsure of, take a step back, give them a little more time, and test them out. This will help you avoid destructive outcomes.

So, why do you make decisions that are based on inaccurate, limited, or distorted observations, thoughts, or assumptions? The reason goes back to your core being disengaged. When your core is disengaged, there is no filter. It allows in all the noise of anything and everyone around you regarding the event. Disengaged, your core's protecting function is impeded. So the things that others do, the things you hear, the things you see, the things you feel, and the things you experience flood in—unchecked by your core. The issues can too easily become clouded, and problems can appear magnified. Inaccurate information floods in resulting in inaccurate assumptions and reactive responses. Then emotions can rise and become excessive. Decisions, then, tend to be heavily impacted by all the noise.

With so much noise coming in, critical information can get lost or distorted, which can confuse and disrupt perception. It can create false assumptions, including the assumption that you are being threatened when you're not. This can result in confused or uncertain goals and priorities. Beware, you can choke on the flood of noise. The more you choke, the more you struggle and fail.

Why You Choke

If you don't engage your core, because of the resulting flood of noise impeding or distorting your observations, cognitions and assumptions and the inevitable resulting rise in emotions, the resulting momentum will keep you making the same mistakes you've made in the past. You may even find yourself making them more persistently and more obsessively.

"I know it did not work last time, but it will this time." "If I just do it one more time." "If I just keep arguing." "If I just keep pleading." "If I just keep fighting." "If I quit and start over one more time." "If I just keep isolating."

It's like being tied up and saying, "If I just pull harder on the rope, I'll get loose."

Little do you know that there is a noose on the other end—and you're in it. The harder you pull, the more you struggle, and ultimately choke. It will eventually destroy you.

Tenet 19

When faced with a negative event, engage your core and perform an OCEANS assessment. Be clear and accurate. Make sure your actions are based on clear observations. Make sure your thoughts are clear and ordered. Make sure you are aware of your emotions and their momentum. Make sure your assumptions are logical, based on fact, and not generalized or exaggerated. Make sure you know which of your need levels are being impacted. Reposition yourself, strategize, and act definitively but cautiously. That will keep you from choking.

Notes

Chapter 12

Lack of Wisdom

(4)

*B*e careful, intellect is often mistaken for wisdom. There is, indeed, a difference between intellect and wisdom and between a correct response and a wise one. The fact is, a person can be exceedingly bright and yet operate very unwisely. It is not unusual for even the brightest people to not understand this distinction. Intellect is acting on fact that is applied to a goal. Wisdom is acting on fact that is melded with principle, intuition, values, consideration of options, and heart—and then applied with consideration of short-term and long-term impact and goals.

It considers the obvious, as well as the not-so-obvious, long and short-term impact of the available options, and then weighs them all. A decision that is only correct may only be so, according to a few, or maybe even one of the criteria that make up wisdom, e.g. a person is late for an important meeting, so he runs all the way, bolting across busy streets to get there on time. It may have been a correct decision because he did get to the meeting on time, but not wise because he might have been killed running across the busy streets. The infusing of wisdom into every part of the OCEANS assessment is critical and will result in far better outcomes.

Tenet 20

When faced with a decision, ask if it is right—and if it is wise!

Notes

Chapter 13

Not Recognizing Your Value

(5)

Questioning your own value during particularly rough times can be excruciatingly painful and can span entire lifetimes. People can be devastated by self-doubt. "I can't do anything right. What have I ever accomplished? What good am I?"

Accomplishment versus Value

Our view of our own value tends to be based upon the things we've done and what we possess. We have been carefully taught to think just that. But these actually are examples of accomplishments, and accomplishments are not value. There is a difference. Accomplishment is determined and reflected by what you do, how good you are at doing it, what you have, and how lucky you are. Further, accomplishment tends to refer to only one or a few objectives and activities. Value is, as I said earlier, protected deep within your core, and is absolute, personal, internal, free from external forces, and can never be taken from you. Value is who you are. It is your heart and your soul. It is the answer that negates all personal doubt.

Defining Your Value

So, what happens when you define your value only, or primarily, in terms of your accomplishments—how much money, status, physical accomplishment, recognition, or fame you have, or have achieved? When you do this, they become your sole determining measures of your value. This is what happens when your core disengages. The pressure, in these cases, can be devastating. You become completely dependent upon how much you have, or don't have, or how much you've done, or have not done, and how others view you, or respond to you. You are apt to become self-conscious, depressed, bitter, defeated, obsessive, or enraged if you are not able to amass enough stuff. This ignores the central reality that your value remains deep inside of you. Your value is not dependent on anyone or anything.

For example, suppose you go to a party, you feel good and look forward to meeting new people. You walk up to several people and they introduce themselves. You tell them what you do for a living, (teacher, grocery store manager, taxi cab driver—whatever). It is apparent by their responses that they aren't impressed. That what you do is not high status enough, perhaps you're not wealthy enough. They seem bored and uninterested. Ultimately, they politely walk away.

You leave the party and feel self-doubt, embarrassment, and humiliation. You may feel insulted or personally attacked. You may become defensive or angry. You may become reactive, which puts you at the greatest possible risk of making rash, destructive, or self-destructive decisions. In those cases, you are not apt to recognize the strengths, goodness and power you have, and the independence from other you have. However, if you feel confident about your value, it makes no difference whether the others liked or respected you or what you do for a living.

Being aware of your own value frees you from concern about how others feel about you. It puts you in a place where you can recognize your efforts, the journey (whether successful, or not), and its role in your growth.

Tenet 21

Consider how others feel about you, but only to the point where you take that information and constructively apply it with a future focus, to your own goals and plans for growth. But do so only after thoughtful consideration of the merit of the others' input. Do not to use it as proof of your value—or lack of it.

Recognizing Your Value

With your core engaged and therefore having an awareness and assurance of your value, while you may be disappointed or frustrated about what the others said or did, and that the others at the party did not appear to care for you, you will not be insulted or mired in feelings of hurt, rejection, anger, embarrassment, self-deprecation, self-consciousness, or bitterness. You cannot be hurt! In fact, you will be free of any personal emotional dependence. You can appreciate the journey and start thinking about your next strategic move toward your future.

In some cases, being rejected may, indeed, have real impact. Your livelihood, reputation, or something else important may be at risk. In these cases, you have to carefully plan your next move with your core engaged so your value not in question. There is no defensiveness, reactiveness, or paralysis to derail you—just pure, focused strategizing. You either stay the course (if there is objective reason to do so), change your approach and plan, or drop the whole idea and move on. What you don't do is take it personally. You don't feel abused, rejected, hurt, embarrassed, or undermined. You don't become bitter. You don't panic. You don't become reactive, and you don't become paralyzed. Why? Because your value is not in the balance. It is not at risk. The event does not determine your value. It only serves as a jumping off point for the next steps toward your growth. Negative input or feelings from others should be considered and used only for growing and reaching your goals.

Consider: A person who has the resources such as money, time, contacts, political clout, and insights might do a very good thing by helping hundreds of people for all the right reasons. But does that person have greater value than the person down on his luck who is scraping to make ends meet, simply so he can feed himself? This individual does not have the resources to do the big things. Instead, his efforts are merely to survive. Does he, therefore, have less value? No! Value is deep inside of him, and you. It's in his heart and in his head, and yours.

Real Deficits, Ineffectiveness, and Value

What about a real deficit that keeps you from achieving or moving forward? Yes, you now know that a lack of accomplishment does not reflect value. But yet, what if you have a deficit that has continually impacted you significantly? You cannot ignore that time and again the deficit is creating a barrier. Maybe it's difficulty retaining or understanding information. Maybe it's difficulty following through. Maybe it's fear. Maybe it's time limitations. Maybe it's a lack of innate talent. Maybe it's a physical condition—your height, your weight, or a disability. Whatever the deficit is, it is impacting your ability to achieve a goal. Therefore, your effectiveness and your ability to function in a specific capacity are lacking, leaving you frustrated, depressed, perhaps angry, frightened, or defeated. Ultimately, lacking accomplishment.

Does this deficit reduce your value? No! But, if you feel you are a failure; if you are feeling defeated, bitter, doomed, or embarrassed, then you are incorrectly measuring your value according to these limitations. When you walk out of a meeting feeling like you are a failure, or if you are obsessing that others think you lack value, then you are incorrectly connecting that event/situation to your value.

Suppose you are a member of a work team, but you couldn't contribute because you couldn't understand the salient points. This is not a lack of personal value. You simply were not effective in that situation. If you don't contribute, you are not an effective contributor to that team. A team needs its members to participate. There is no denying that.

But … while you can't be effective to the group if you don't contribute, by engaging your core and recognizing your value, you can use the resulting energy to overcome the effectiveness barrier. Engaging your core and recognizing your value will provide you the vision, energy, options, focus, and actions you need to compensate for any deficits you have.

If it's fear of saying something stupid; not knowing the facts sufficiently; fearing others will criticize you; or being uncomfortable publicizing your perspective, then engaging your core will help you to objectively organize and process your thoughts for logic and accuracy. Then you will be able to develop a solid strategy and identify tools. In this case, perhaps using bullet-pointed fact sheets (and being comfortable using them) to help you communicate with confidence. Or perhaps to objectively recognize that this team is not for you, and decide to move on to something else that is a better fit.

The Transcendence of Value

Value, housed forever safely in your core is transcendent. It crosses all events, issues, people, and time. It serves as a foundation that maintains itself even when things don't go right. You can always rely on this foundation and build your future instead of stewing on the past or floundering in the present. Your value is found deep within your core, and your core is invulnerable.

When you recognize your value is safe in your core, you no longer perform to prove or increase your value. Instead, you perform to accomplish and grow. This reduces the pressure. Have you ever found yourself trying hard to achieve a goal, but the harder you tried, the worse you did? This tends to occur when there is too much at stake. When winning means you have value and losing means you don't. Then defensiveness kicks in. Emotion takes over. Desperation sets in. You overcompensate in terms of energy, pressure, speed, tension, and worry. Remember the noose? The result is that you choke.

Tenet 22

The fact that others may feel you have no value due to your ineffectiveness is not part of your equation. Don't put it in there. The activities that reflect your effectiveness (or lack of it) are exclusively the tools you use to reach your goals and grow. Any negative event can help you grow if your core is engaged. Again, your value is never at stake. So, use those positive and negative events to grow.

Notes

Searching, Demanding or Begging For Respect, Relevance, Significance, and Validation

(6)

*T*here are times in most people's lives when they look for validation from others. Times when maybe we just need a sign from others that we are okay. Times when we are feeling unsure of who we are and what value we hold. This is not unusual. Most of us do it at one time or another. However, when your desire for validation from others becomes your need for validation from others. When this need seems to always be there. If you're actually measuring your value by the extent to which others do validate you, then you, too easily can be left with disappointment, bitterness, self-consciousness, insecurity, self-loathing, and a sense of insignificance, when they don't.

Further, when proving yourself moves from demonstrating your effectiveness (getting a job, being picked for the team, or selling an idea) to defending or proving your value (your worth, your right to exist, your being deserving of respect), it becomes a problem. In those cases, you are apt to obsess about the fear of losing your value instead of the task at hand. Instead, focus on your own goals and spend time and effort on your growth-oriented activities, happiness, and satisfaction. If you don't, ultimately, you can become mired in insecurity, self-loathing, frustration, anger, defensiveness, depression, and fear of failing. You cannot find your place if your focus is on demanding, begging, or expecting others to value you.

This need for value from others may be completely subconscious. Don't say you don't have that need before you consider it very carefully.

Example: Thomas picked up Jean for their date. Jean was uncomfortable most of the evening. Finally, Thomas asked her what the matter was. After some hesitation, she told him she was breaking up with him. With significant prodding, she told Thomas that she was looking for someone with more ambition (money). Thomas was devastated. He dropped her off and then spent the rest of his life driving himself to make as much money as possible.

Thomas eventually did make a huge amount of money, but he was never really invested in what he was doing. He was never happy, satisfied, or secure since he was trying to earn his value from others, (specifically from Jean, though she walked out of his life long ago). Therefore, he always questioned himself and his value. To him his value was dependent on how much money he had, but even the money could not give him the sense of value and security he sought. He always was searching for something more. He died a wealthy, but very unhappy, man.

The problem with this, is that when you do not see your own value and instead you look for it through the reactions and recognition of others, you lose your balance and your focus. This is because, in these cases, only *their* recognition of your value proves to you that you have it. But, then you can easily become obsessed with trying to find ways to be valued by others, and then too easily become devastated when they don't.

When you can't generate your own sense of value internally—it is because your core is not engaged. Then all you can do is look for your value from others. Then, when others do not recognize your value, you have five choices:

First, you can demand that others value you. In this case, the tendency is to assert your right to be respected and to be considered relevant, significant, valuable and competent by others. Then, if you don't get it, you assert your authority, or your strength by becoming angry, frustrated, punishing, threatening, sarcastic, vindictive, or perhaps even violent. Or you may decide to completely disassociate from those who don't value you. Keep in mind, when your need to be respected or valued by others becomes too strong, it is your own personal insecurities about your own value resulting from your disengaged core that is causing it.

A typical dictator defines his value by the amount of power he has over others. The proof of his value is in his ability to get them to do his bidding. He tends to do so through threats and force—often without boundaries or limitations. In reality, genuine respect and validation cannot be gained through artificial means such as promoting fear through force, pressure, punishment, deception, or coercion. Don't try it. The dictator is always reacting to his own paranoia and insecurities. His actions are always fueled by his greed and insecurity, and he doesn't care if the respect is genuine as long as he gets what he wants—power, wealth, adulation and legacy. If he defined his value internally, he would not need to hold power over others and force others to make him wealthy and powerful because his value would not be defined by those things.

Second, you can try hard to prove your value to others. However, proving can quickly become groping and begging, which are signs of desperation, and desperation can too easily cause you to act rashly and become obsessive, which tends to result in pity or rejection by others. Remember, you never have to prove your value. You have it and that is all that is important.

Third, you can punish yourself emotionally or physically for not succeeding in getting others to recognize your value. This is often cloaked in self-destructive or self-defeating behaviors like drinking to excess or continually berating yourself for your failures. This never brings about respect from others. It only damages you and certainly does nothing to build your value.

In these three situations, you can become so desperate that you select destructive or self-destructive shortcuts to quickly prove your value. This is often done by cheating, forcing others, theft, begging for forgiveness, punishing others, demanding validation, demanding second chances, or taking unwise risks to try to rush a change in the perspectives of others. Why do you select destructive or self-destructive ways? You do so because they are typically faster and more direct, especially when you want to fix an event before word gets out, before more damage is done, before you lose, or before you sink even lower in despair. You do so when you need to expel frustration—now! You do so when you need to justify yourself and prove yourself so that everyone knows—now! Shortcuts can be attractive options, but quick fixes seldom work. They often provide only limited and temporary improvement, and they often cause more problems. Finally, they also stunt the potential for real growth.

Fourth, you can accept not having others recognize your value—at least for now. This can be positive as long as you don't become generally passive or lower your standards to the point where you cease trying to grow. "It doesn't matter. I really didn't want it that bad. Nothing I would do would make them respect me anyway."

NOTE: Remember, all of these responses are actually manifestations of your insecurities and a disengaged core. This may surprise you. But it's true. When you feel like demanding or proving your value to others, or punishing yourself for not getting others to value you, or just giving up, in general, think about this last statement and step back.

Fifth, (and best). You can engage and nurture your core. Focus only on engaging your core. Focus on your goals and your future—and not on what others do, say or feel. You will feel and know your value. Positive responses from others are apt to come later, but keep in mind their recognition of your value isn't required for you to have value. You already have value.

Keep in mind, being valued by others should be the result of your efforts, never the focus of your efforts. The difference is when you focus your efforts on being valued, the tendency is to operate defensively, and take shortcuts and look for it too soon, from the wrong people, for the wrong reasons, in the wrong ways, and at the wrong times. Your efforts should be expressions of your growth—not forces that demand or plead for others to value you. Nor should they be to punish others, or yourself, for their failure to do so.

Your goal, in these cases, should be to realize you have value regardless of what others think and regardless of what you've done. If you set out to prove your value by trying to elicit a positive reaction, opinion, or statement from others by demanding, pleading, bribing, obsessing, punishing, manipulating, justifying, defending, re-explaining, reframing, or disavowing something you did, it is apt to lead to self-destruction. You do not have to prove your value to anyone.

Your Need for Others to Value You

So, why is it so important to us that others believe we have value? Why is it so important that they see us as important, significant, relevant, competent, or capable? And why is it so disruptive to us when they don't? We can become so easily angered, hurt, depressed, or defensive. This may sound presumptuous, but it is true of most of us. So I'll assume you are no different. It hits us so hard because we often use being valued by others, though inaccurately, as our primary measure of our own value. We do something we think is good, then we look back to see if we are recognized as having value. We love the recognition, the applause, the rewards, the money, the adulation, and the fame … who doesn't? Then, if we don't get it, it crushes us—and we question our value.

This goes right to the heart of Maslow's self-concept need level. It is perhaps the most disruptive and emotionally painful need when unmet. That is why it hurts so badly when we feel we are not getting it. That's also why some people go to such extremes to get it, and sometimes they go to such extremes to blame and punish those who don't give it to them. But as I said, these are not true measures of our value. They are artificial measures. Let me ask you this: Does a wealthy, successful celebrity who is adored by millions have more value than a poor single womn living on welfare who has no following? No!! In fact, in many cases, the poor live what many would feel are far more meaningful lives, recognizing, attending to, and being thankful for the simple things.

Should being valued by others be a concern of yours? Whether you answer yes, or no, it's usually a reality. Since you live in a world with others, this, understandably, is apt to be important to you. While there are times when you have to do what you feel is right regardless of what others say, or think, usually you do want to be accepted and valued by them. (Just keep in mind, once again, your being valued by others does not, in any manner, define or determine your value. I want to repeat this because it is so important: Your being valued by others does not, in any manner, define or determine your value.)

Tenet 23

Don't demand, beg for, or expect others to give you validation or respect, or recognize your relevance, competency, or significance—in other words, your value. Don't base your actions on getting their endorsements. Work only on your goals and on your growth—engage your core. The validation of others is apt to follow.

Tenet 24

You may demonstrate proficiency, talent, and sincerity to others— but never your value. Your value is there and does not need to be proved.

Let Them Think, Say and Do What They Will

The fact is, what others say or think about you is irrelevant. Who cares? If you like what they say or think, fine. If not, you have three options: ignore it and move on, be beaten by it, or change it. If you choose to ignore it, then ignore it. Let … it … go. If you choose to be beaten by it, blame no one. It is your decision. If you choose to change it, make your plan. But make sure the plan focuses on your long-term growth and nurturing the goals that are really important to you. Don't attempt to quickly convince, force, alter, beg, bribe, or coerce others into changing their opinions about you, and make sure your plan is not an attempt to punish them when they won't.

You now understand that it is not what people do, say, or think that determines your value. They are tools that you can use to become stronger, better, and happier. They are tools to help you grow. But you must fully understand and internalize this to avoid getting caught up in, and disrupted by, the things people do, say, and think about you. You have to actually program yourself to immediately look beyond the things people do, say, or think. You must respond intellectually, wisely, and independent of emotion and hurt. You have to respond, not react. You have to use the things they do, say, and think—even the negative things—to nurture your growth and meet your goals. Don't let them disrupt you, manipulate you, hurt you, or define your value.

Ultimately, let them be mad. It won't kill you. Let them think you're wrong. It won't kill you. Let them think you're missing the point, the boat, or even some marbles. It won't kill you. Let them not think about you at all. It won't kill you! It's okay.

The tendency will be to try to to, or at least want to, convince them that you are right, smart, good, or talented. You might let it hurt you or defeat you. But, unless your life, job, home, or family depends upon it, right now, let it go! I know it's maddening. I know that it gnaws at you. I know you see them with their knowing little leers, smiles, expressions of disgust, and dismissive attitudes. Who cares? Let it go! Just let it go. The more you don't try to fix it, the better chance you have of doing so. You can fix it by going back to your own plan for growth. Reposition yourself strategically, if necessary, and then, act. Do not react. Do not shrink back and do not adjust solely to get them to change their minds. Adjust only to grow your future according to your plan.

Tenet 25

If it's not imperative, let them think, say, and do what they will. If your life, job, home, or family does depend upon it, respond objectively, wisely and strategically. But, don't always try to do and say the right thing simply to please others or have them give you value. Don't focus on what people think, say, or do. Focus on what you need to do now to reach your goal—to grow.

NOTE: I am not suggesting you should not listen to what others are saying to, or about you. It is important that we all listen and reflect on what is being done, thought or said about, or to us—even if we do not like it. But, if you have considered others' perspectives and objectively determined that your perspective is the correct and wise one, then let it go.

Notes

Chapter 15

Adolescents—Value, and Peer Pressure (Special Considerations)

(7)

The ideas presented in this book can be effectively applied to adolescents, but there are several additional considerations.

Just as with adults, knowing they are valued is also very important to teens. Adolescents often will go to great lengths to prove their value, particularly to their peers. But, they too often allow themselves to be drawn into unhealthy, counterproductive, sometimes even dangerous activities in order to be accepted—to prove their value to their peers. Why are they particularly susceptible to the influences of their peers?

For many adolescents, immediacy drives their actions. The desire to be valued now is paramount. This being the case, the quickest way to gain this recognition is to make loud statements—actions that are powerful, rebellious, shocking and sometimes even dangerous or destructive. This is often believed to be the quickest way to be seen as courageous, clever, able and accepted—valued.

What complicates things is that their ability to clearly examine issues, risks, priorities, short-term and particularly longer-term repercussions of their actions are still developing, so, it is not uncommon for them to act or react in ways that might ultimately harm them, their goals, or others.

Adolescents do not yet have the experience, which is simply a function of having only lived a very few years, on which to make comparisons or draw on history as a guide to making sound decisions.

Since they have not yet fully developed the ability to engage their cores, many adolescents are often not yet able to resist looking to their peers to define their value. They don't recognize that their value is already a reality and, because of this, they are unable to focus on their growth, independently and wisely, to launch their futures.

An additional consideration is that some kids (bullies) can be extremely punitive if they perceive that one of their peers is of less value. This can result in greater susceptibility of kids to be bullied and/or drawn into dangerous activities in order to avoid further punishment. This susceptibility is, in part, due to limited perspective, lack of experience and difficulty identifying options as to how to escape this punishment. (Keep in mind, bullies, bully as a result of their own insecurities and damaged self-concept, and the need to prove their own worth by beating down others—indicating an unengaged core.

There are whole books written about adolescent behaviors that go into great detail that are definitely worth reading. This book provides a glimpse into several key insights that will help them look deeply into themselves and help those working with them.

So as you read this book—either as an adult who is attempting to better understand teens, or as a teen who is trying to better understand your own actions and feelings—recognize that these influences are part of the equation and need to be understood and dealt with.

Notes

Chapter 16

Trying to Undo a Past Event

(8)

*T*ake a look at this example: John agreed to participate on a panel to discuss new advancements in computer equipment. As soon as the discussion started, John found he was not prepared and offered very little input. After the discussion was over, he left quietly. He was embarrassed at his lack of competence. As the rest of the evening wore on, he began to stew about how the others must have perceived him as incompetent. So he decided to set them straight.

The next day, he called the other panel members and several people from the audience he knew and gave them all sorts of pertinent information he had put together since the panel met. He also offered excuses for why he was not on his game. The problem is that he's trying to undo an event that had already taken place. This tends to cause more problems than it solves. It focuses others on the unfortunate incident and it engrains his past disappointment in his own mind. Don't try to undo an event. It cannot be undone.

Attempts at undoing typically fail miserably. Why? Because, first, undoing typically breeds overcompensating and overdoing it. Second, undoing creates an artificial and pressured exchange that is often transparent to the other person. It becomes an obvious and awkward conversation Third, you're bringing more attention to the event than was there in the first place. Finally, it is self-sabotaging in that it reinforces to you the idea that you are indeed lessened in value by an event or the others' perception of you.

Trying to undo is like trying to uncrack an egg. It gets messy and more obviously, it's impossible. It's better to take the cracked egg and go from there. Find a way to use it. Scramble it, fry it, poach it, bake a cake with it, or come up with a new way of using it. Or freeze it until you can think of a new idea, a new approach, a new target, and a new strategy. That will make good use of that egg.

It is true that, at times, a situation needs to be strategically rectified. But this is only when such a rectification can bring about a positive next event. The difference between undoing and strategically rectifying a situation is that strategically rectifying a situation is an objective, intellectual and wisdom-based strategic process with a future-oriented goal. Here, a situation is identified, the problem is defined, a pivotal event is identified, and potential responses are considered. Clarifying a past statement, or action to correct, or avoid a substantive error that otherwise may do damage may be considered as well. Such rectification could include creating or adjusting the next positive growth-oriented event. Then, selecting the best response.

Undoing, on the other hand, is an emotional reaction that is typically a shortsighted attempt at a poorly planned quick fix, or a futile attempt to replay and abruptly change what has already happened, or change how people view it. Strategically rectifying creates a future-oriented opportunity for lasting positive change. Undoing is a defensive reaction based on an insecurity inside of you, and it usually results in dismissiveness, confusion, aggravation, ambivalence, suspicion, avoidance, or pity because others can see what you're trying to do.

If John didn't immediately let them know why he wasn't on his game, or let them know he is, indeed, intelligent, they may consider him inept. This could cause him to miss out on future opportunities. But, instead of calling all the panelists and audience members and slamming them with facts and figures to impress them, or clumsily explaining his lack of performance, he could have been far more successful looking at the next opportunity for growth. He could have learned the material better, or better prepared himself for the next opportunity to communicate his knowledge. He may need to be creative in identifying his next opportunity.

Tenet 26

Trying to undo an event typically creates more of a problem than you started with. Don't focus on the past—and certainly don't try to undo it. Instead, focus strategically on your next step toward your future.

Notes

Chapter 17

Letting Your Ego Drive You

(9)

Your emotions are high, and defensiveness is driving you. It's also driving your pride and your sense of value. Something inside tells you that you can't just let it go. What will people think? What will you think? What about your reputation? You can't be thought of as weak, stupid, or naïve. If your core is engaged, your ego has two key functions. It helps you recognize your own value in order to keep you strong, forward thinking, and growing. It also maintains and protects you when your value is questioned, challenged, threatened, or doubted by others, or by you. It helps you maintain a positive perspective of yourself. It keeps you strong, focused on the future, and motivated to grow.

This is important in order to make sure that you keep yourself safe and that you keep meeting your needs. If your core is engaged, your ego maintains a balance with a positive outlook, yet not pulling so hard as to run your life with pomposity, arrogance, rashness, or defensiveness.

The Ego Rush

But there is another side of the ego. If your core is not engaged, its measured protective element is interrupted, so your ego can be easily thrown into a high defensive mode and may detect a threat to your value that does not exist. When the perceived threat is severe, the tendency is to react emotionally, impulsively, defensively, and aggressively.

These ego rushes occur when your ego is triggered and kicked into gear specifically to prove your value at the expense of wisdom—potentially at the expense of others' feelings or well-being and without regard to any potential fallout from its actions. An ego rush and its bases may be completely out of your conscious awareness. The result is that the ego can kick in, push too hard, yell too loud, and self-protect too aggressively, all without you being aware of it. An overly active ego can brag, boast, strut, behave rashly, attack, argue, avenge, and refuse to give in or admit flaws. It ignores others' feelings and well-being and the potential long-term, or peripheral impact of its resulting actions.

When your core is not engaged, your ego can also draw out emotions that actually make you feel weak, useless, or victimized when you feel others are looking down on you, when they do not see you as competent or desirable, or when they are not taking you seriously. Similarly, when you consciously or subconsciously feel that there is no chance of changing these people's perspectives, your ego can draw out depression, anxiety and despair. All this, again, to warn you and protect you—but in very damaging ways.

NOTE: Some people's egos rush pretty much continuously, such as those who are perpetual braggarts and those who are in a state of perpetual defensiveness.

Ego or Substance

When you are feeling highly emotional, being able to identify your feeling as one of substance or ego is a critical ability that, without it, can cause you to make major mistakes in your responses.

How can you tell the difference? How can you tell that what you are feeling is simply a reaction to a (misguided) perception of lost value? In other words, a bruised ego, that should not be reacted to, but instead, just identified, worked through, or put aside, as opposed to an objective response to a substantive situation. To tell the difference, you have to ask; is there any real actual or potential practical damage (damage that has a specific negative measurable impact on a specific goal) as a result of the situation? Rate the actual or potential damage one to ten (one is no damage and ten is critical damage). Then identify how bothered you are. You can rate your distress from one to ten, as well. If the actual, or potential practical damage is minimal but your distress is high, then your ego is rushing. Put it aside. If the actual, or potential practical damage is high, respond to that. The key is to separate the ego rush and its issues from practical damage. Attending only to the practical damage deenergizes the rush and keeps you focused on growth and goal-oriented actions.

Example: You walk into an electronics store with your computer that stopped working. You tell the tech your computer hasn't worked for three days. The tech plugs the cord in the wall, looks at the side of the computer, and pushes the other end further into the port. It starts right up. He gives you that "aren't you stupid" little smile. You thank him and walk away. After a little more shopping, you pass by him and you hear him telling another tech about how stupid that customer was to not know enough to push the plug into the computer all the way. You feel stupid, inept, a little embarrassed and angry.

Substance or ego? Ask yourself if there is any practical damage to you, or to anything, or anyone that matters? If not, then it's ego. If yes, then it's substance. In this case, it is ego. There is no practical damage. As always, your value is not at risk. Let it go. It does not matter. Your only attention to the event should be asking, "What can I learn from this?" Answer—plug in the cord all the way, and in general, be sure you have checked everything out.

If you feel it's important to let the tech or his manager know how rude he was, do so—but only to assert your right to be treated appropriately. Don't be dependent on getting the tech to see things your way, apologize, or recognize your value. It may not happen, and you don't need it to happen.

Tenet 27

You have to be aware of whether you are reacting to substance or an ego rush. In some cases, it can be a combination. If it is, separate the two, identify both, and attend only to the substance-based, actual, or potential practical damage.

Let them think, do, and say what they will. Keep in mind a bruised ego will try to trick you into thinking it's substantive. Don't be tricked into thinking you are experiencing—or will experience—actual damage when it isn't likely to happen. Just ask, "What can I learn from this?" Then move on.

Notes

Chapter 18

Getting Defensive

(10)

The discussion about our egos spoke of defensiveness. Now, let's look closely at what defensiveness actually is. There are times when you have to defend yourself. In fact, all behaviors are defending tools. They are always ensuring that some need is met. We all do it. There are times when assertively defending yourself is appropriate for keeping you from being hurt or defending an important position you hold. But, when defending yourself becomes defending your value, relevance, or significance, it becomes defensiveness. Defending defends position, decisions, specific practical goals, people, belongings, practical safety, philosophy, or principle. Defensiveness defends value. When you become defensive, you are defending something that does not need defending—your value.

Acting defensively impacts you in several ways. First, it is time-consuming and exhausting. Second, over time, it breeds further insecurities. It does so because you become programmed to be constantly on alert for those who might attack or doubt your value. Third, defensiveness is most-often gilded with emotion, often heightened or out-of-control so your reactions can be rash, counterproductive, or damaging. In addition, others tend to see this defensiveness as weakness and irrationality. It can undermine your reputation, your position, your status, your credibility, and your efforts. Finally, it distracts from the real issue at hand. The rule is, defend yourself in order to accomplish or support a practical goal, a position, a decision, people, belongings, tasks, your safety, a philosophy, or a principle. Do not defend to prove or protect your value. And realize that sometimes it's difficult to know the difference.

NOTE: Beware, sometimes your emotions can be internal and may not show up outwardly. You may not be fully conscious of their existence during the situation at hand. When you effectively defend your goal, position, decision, safety, philosophy, people, or principle, then your value, competency, relevance, or significance will stand the best chance of being noticed. Remember, the function of defending is to communicate and reposition strategically. It is not to prove your value or compel others to see it. You defend most effectively by, first, performing an OCEANS assessment.

Tenet 28

Defend—but do not become defensive. Defending defends practical goals, position, decisions, practical issues, safety, actions, people, belongings, philosophies, or principles. Defensiveness defends value. You must ask yourself: "Am I defending, or am I being defensive?" If you are being defensive, engage your core, perform an OCEANS assessment, and stop trying to prove your value.

NOTE: Keep in mind that even when defending something important to you, it is important that you continually assess the situation and consider if and when it is in your best interest to stop defending. Weigh out the comparative harm/implications of continuing to defend versus moving on.

Notes

Chapter 19

Searching for Wholeness

(11)

Some people mourn their entire lives because they feel empty. They feel something's missing. They feel unfulfilled. Wholeness, for some, seems unobtainable, particularly when they feel they are not valued by others and they, themselves, do not feel they have value. The desire to be whole is a universal one that keeps us all searching and striving. Without this striving, we would become stagnant. There is, however, an error in thought here. For in fact, we all are whole.

But the fact that you are whole does not mean you do not search. Being whole does not mean you don't have any unmet needs, goals, or desires. Being whole does not mean you have everything you want.

Being whole means recognizing that searching is part of being whole. It's not a way to get there. It is the search—the journey—that completes you. As long as you search, you are whole. It is only when you give up and stop searching that you stagnate, or concede defeat and lose a critical part of you. You lose your wholeness.

You are a dynamic being who becomes stronger through your search. You are whole through your search. Being whole means being whole in value and meaning. Being whole means searching, not to prove yourself, not for value. not for wholeness, but searching for long-term and short-term growth opportunities through trial and error, success and failure, and through accomplishments—big and small. Searching, which you should do until the day you die. Enjoy every second of your search. Enjoy your wholeness.

Engaging your core and searching for growth every day of your life, cements the knowledge that you are, indeed, whole, and it allows you to enjoy that feeling.

NOTE: Even people who do feel whole still search, but they do not feel their value is dependent upon finding any particular answer. So there is no desperation.

Wholeness and Loss

You may have felt the wrenching gasping for air that comes from realizing something or someone you desperately wanted, loved, or needed, will never be there for you again. We're talking about the feeling that life for you is ending, or the realization that life will continue to happen, but it will drag you with it like a child drags a rag doll along a concrete sidewalk, not looking back to see it bouncing, scuffing, and ripping against the harsh pavement.

Why does the absence or loss of a certain person or a certain thing bring you such devastation? It goes back to the issue of wholeness, value, and belonging, and the perceived loss of that wholeness, value, and belonging. It is the emotional, sometimes subconscious, assumption that without that person or thing, you are not whole; that you have lost an absolutely critical part of what you require to live; that you have less value; that you have less potential; that you are less worthy. You don't necessarily believe it intellectually, but you react to it emotionally as if you do. It throws you right into the foundation need levels of belonging and self-concept. It can be as painful and real as someone tearing off your arm or taking your eyes. The fact is, however, even with loss, you are whole. Do you hurt when you suffer a loss? Certainly, but with your core engaged, you have not lost your wholeness, your personhood, your balance, your potential, or your value, And—You—Know—That!

Therefore, you still have the capacity to have a vision for the future. Then, the pain, while it still may be there, does not cut nearly as deep.

Example: There was a man at a conference on grief I attended years ago. He stood up and he began to cry as he told us about the death of wife. He told us he was experiencing excruciating sadness and that every day of his life was torture. The unexpected part of this story is that she had died more than twenty years earlier, yet the pain had not subsided. He had never been able to adjust to a life without her. He could not adjust because he had not engaged his core, therefore he could not use his core to protect him from the intense and relentless feelings of loss. There was no sense of wholeness, strength, or value. There was no possibility of moving on with his life without her. There was no vision of his future and no energy to grow with. Therefore, he was stuck and he remained devastated.

Wholeness and Loneliness

Long nights, feeling like you are on the outside of the world looking in. Longing for connectedness. Enduring desolation that never seems to end. Here, we are not talking about the person who feels a little bummed that there's no one to go out with this Saturday night. We are talking about the agony that devastates. That incessant loneliness that seems to go on year after year with gnawing that just won't stop, and with coldness that creeps into your bones, your head, and your heart.

True loneliness, in fact, has nothing to do with having someone to be with. You know that because you can feel that loneliness in a room full of people. Persistent and relentless loneliness is actually the epitome of perceived loss of wholeness.

It occurs when there is a total loss of yourself. It occurs when any sense of wholeness is absent, leaving you feeling that you are nothing more than a shell of what you were meant to be—what you want to be. It is a feeling of emptiness, vulnerability, and worthlessness—loss of value.

The understandable reaction to loneliness is a desperate search for wholeness. Its most dire forms include obsessively trying to salvage a relationship that has broken up, imagining a relationship that was never there, entering into immediate new relationships—even if they are unhealthy ones; obsessing on the loneliness, lashing out, or pulling in, in isolation and depression; and possibly even having suicidal thoughts.

While loneliness, at its core, is not about having someone to be with, it is exactly that, which you often yearn for when you are experiencing true loneliness. At these times you want to be loved—you yearn for it. You yearn to have that special person—a soul mate—with whom you can connect because it is that connection that makes you feel whole. It gives you the feeling of completeness. Not only that, it can become your belief that it is that connection that gives you, and proves to you (and others), your value.

So what should you do when that loneliness sets in? The answer is twofold. First, engage your core. Second, respond to your foundation need for belonging. You do this by forming connections—and not by groping for that one specific illusive connection or groping for love. Looking for love, in these cases, is specific, one-dimensional, artificial, desperate, and reactive. Connecting is broad, proactive and multifaceted. It comes from a position of strength. The connection may be with other people or with an activity, a cause, a task, a career, or a belief. Whatever form it takes to connect you with some aspect of the world around you, do it! Even though your heart won't be in it, do it! The worst thing you can do is resist connecting with anyone or anything other than the one person or thing you lost, or waiting until you find that one single person or thing you are yearning for.

Wholeness and Love

We can't talk about wholeness without talking about love. Love is probably the most vexing and perplexing occurrence in the human experience. While it certainly can provide utter ecstasy, it can also be devastating. Why is it that so many of us have fallen in love and then have been so devastatingly disrupted when it did not work out?

Was the person who was the focus of our love truly so remarkable, wonderful, beautiful, handsome, bright, talented, giving, or otherwise more fabulous than anyone else? Was this person truly the only one out there who could meet our needs and desires? Because if this is true, then it is also true that we will never find anyone else who measures up. But the fact is, over time, most of us who have loved and lost have found someone else. While it seemed so at the time, the person who we once saw as perfect for us and just plain perfect, period, no longer seems so. But in these cases, it isn't usually the person who changes, it is our perspective that changes. Do we simply chalk up the "I'll never find another" perspective, to that love is blind cliché, where all we see is the positive and not the negative? I don't think so.

while i am not arguing that love can and does often blind us. that particular insight does not help us understand our blindness, and it certainly does not help us when we are in the midst of a love-based emotional crash. if anything, we deny our blindness at the time, and it only makes us feel stupid when we recognize it later. most importantly, it does not adequately explain these feelings.

so why do you tune in to one specific person and hurt so badly when he or she is gone? let's break this down to very basic concepts. when you are in love, the tendency is to subconsciously reduce the engagement of your core. in some cases, you might totally disengage your core. here, you lower all your defenses. why? it goes back to the basic need for connectedness, and the ultimate connection is when you lower all defenses (you disengage your core) and let someone else connect with you so completely that he or she becomes part of you. that's love. two minds, souls, hearts, and bodies become one. it's a wonderful thing. it's romantic, poetic, and exciting. it is also, to an extent, desirable and necessary in order to let someone get close to you in a loving relationship. but it also puts you at tremendous risk. because when one person leaves the relationship, it rips the joined heart, soul, mind, and body apart.

note: if you ever had an incision from surgery and let it almost heal, then inadvertently pull the two flaps of skin apart, you know the excruciating physical pain that results. the same is true of love lost and emotional pain.

Why We Love Who We Love

When we experience this kind of love and loss, we can become desperate for that one specific person—over all others. Why is this? It is because we see something (perhaps subconsciously) in that person that we feel gives us what we lack. The person who feels unimportant may gravitate to someone who the world (or some part of it) sees as important, or who he feels will make him feel important. The person who feels weak may gravitate to someone who she feels strengthens her or makes her feel safe. Someone who feels insignificant may gravitate to someone who is very accomplished or well-known, or who she simply feels is significant. In other words, the person gives us what we feel we do not have or what we want more of. That person, in effect, makes us whole. The logical assumption, then, is that, without this person, we are not whole. We are incomplete. In the extreme, we are defective. We are like a machine missing a critical part.

So, if this is happening to you, this belief that you are incomplete can be devastating. But, if you can break down that overwhelming feeling of love into concrete thoughts, you will be able to objectively define your feelings and then begin to understand them and respond to them strategically, and then move on.

Exactly when this need becomes love and exactly what love is, are questions that are not well-understood. No one knows. Maybe it's that moment when needs, desires, and wholeness all merge. Or maybe it's when we find an individual who seems to fill our self-actualization needs as well as portions of the other need levels to create ultimate desire. I also suggest that we allow for the possibility that the illusive mystical occurrence of love is something that is just not supposed to be dissected or defined. Suffice it to say that, whether it's need or love, considering these issues can help you through these very painful moments.

Why We Love People Who Aren't Good for Us

So, why is it that some people are attracted to people who behave badly? Abusers, gamblers, cheaters, the self-absorbed and drug abusers are just a few who, somehow, attract even good and intelligent people. There are several possible reasons. Bad behaviors can seem adventurous, intriguing, and exciting. Getting involved with those who sport bad behaviors, particularly who are disapproved of by parents, or others, can be a statement of independence. Daring to behave badly can be interpreted as strength, courage, or intellect—attractive characteristics. Sometimes, people attracted to those who behave badly may feel like they deserve someone like that. So, why do we hold on so tightly—even to someone who behaves badly? Bad behavior or not, we hold on harder in order to not lose the part of them that we believe makes us whole. Without them, we would be left with part of us ripped out. We'd be left incomplete.

NOTE: There are two other possibilities for why we hold on to someone who is bad for us.

1. We do not feel we have the ability to get anyone better.
2. We are afraid of being physically punished if we try to leave. In this situation, we need to seek help because no one should endure abuse.

NOTE: When our cores disengage, wisdom and intellect no longer are able to fully function. That leaves us with emotional and potentially erratic responses.

When the Desperation Is Gone

With time, the pain and devastation resulting from a loss usually subside. Maybe you just accept the loss internally or maybe you finally meet someone else and you begin to enjoy the new possibilities. How does that happen? Why do you no longer hurt? It's because you finally are able to engage your core again. You aren't dependent on that person you lost for wholeness and value. Your core fills that need—not the person. With your core engaged, you may still feel sad but you will not feel the devastation. You will not be stuck in the past or paralyzed in the present. You will be focused on the future.

The problem is that too often your core is sluggish. It takes time to engage, especially after it has been dormant which occurs when you let someone you love in (as we talked about earlier), or you assumed for a long time (perhaps subconsciously) that the person gave you your value and your wholeness. Beware, even in the midst of a great relationship, your core may become disengaged. Keep in touch with your core. Keep it engaged—even when times are good.

So, what can you do to avoid drowning in the pain of lost love? There are three things that will help:

1. Prior to identifying that you are in love with a specific person, keep your core engaged as much as possible. Feel your wholeness and your value every day. This keeps you open to others but strong enough to not misinterpret the role they will play. Be constantly aware of the fact that no other person will not make you whole. You are already whole.

2. When you first identify that you are in love with a specific person, check that your core is engaged. Make a conscious effort to state (to yourself) what this person is and isn't. "She is beautiful, fun, and talented, and I want to be with her. However, she is not my value and she does not and cannot make me whole. I have value, and I am whole with or without her." Then maintain balance by, along with the things you do together and the interest you share, maintaining your own interests, friends, and activities (separate from the other person).

   Note: This does not do away with the idea or reality of romance. You can still adore someone, want to spend the rest of your life with him or her, and feel your life is infinitely richer with that person. However, you can do so without giving away your value and wholeness to that person.

3. After a relationship goes bad, make sure your core is engaged. If it isn't, then engage it ASAP (and it may be tough). Feel your value and your wholeness. Recognize that they are still there, undamaged and unchanged.

NOTE: I revisit the experience of loss and death in appendix 1 since it can be such a powerful, life-changing event. If after reading this section on wholeness and loss, feel free to jump to the appendix. I go into much more depth about how to interpret loss and deal with it. After reading the appendix, come back to read the rest of the book.

What Does Wholeness Feel Like?

The wholeness you are looking for may best be described as a sense of contentment. Not a sense that you have everything you want, but that the search is no longer undesirable—it is embraced. The sense that the search is no longer the antithesis of wholeness. You still have unattained goals, but they do not represent failure, incompetence, lack of wholeness, or lack of value. They represent potential for further growth.

The feeling of wholeness may initially be fleeting. It may be a momentary chance to exhale. It may be five seconds where you say to yourself, "For just a few seconds, I didn't hurt. I didn't yearn." It may be gone as quickly as it came, but you are beginning to engage your core. Recognize it, feel it, taste it, and savor it. Remember, while it may be a fleeting moment, it is a critical accomplishment. That is what you are looking for. That moment is your core engaging.

Tenet 29

You are whole today, you were whole yesterday, and you will be whole tomorrow. Your wholeness is there. It does not come from situations or from what people give you, feel about you, say about you, do to you, or do for you. The world does not make you whole.

The world gives you unlimited opportunities for growth and ways to express your wholeness. Recognize the world as such and take the opportunities.

Tenet 30

It is the searching, itself, that makes you whole, not the result of the search. Succeed or fail. If you searched, you grew from it. You are whole.

Notes

Chapter 20

Denying Errors, Flaws, Bad Experiences, Regrets, and Failures

(12)

*Y*ou make an error. It eats at you. Maybe it was your fault—and maybe it wasn't. Maybe you tell yourself it wasn't your fault, that you had no choice, or you had every right to do what you did. But it doesn't help. It still eats at you. You go back and forth, blaming others, blaming yourself, denying what you did, or justifying why you did what you did. But it still eats at you. The error follows you relentlessly for years.

Errors, flaws, bad experiences, regrettable decisions, and failures, all too often are denied realities that can haunt and sabotage your life. They have the ability to gnaw at you, chew you up, beat you down, paralyze you, and ultimately keep you from finding your place.

Errors, flaws, bad experiences, regrettable decisions, and failures are called denied realities because people are apt to want to forget (deny their existence) or justify (deny responsibility or blame).

So, what should you do when these denied realities occur and you absolutely can't get past them? What you don't do is get stuck denying them by justifying, explaining, rationalizing, hiding, defending, or excusing them. Don't blame others, or beat or blame yourself for them. Blaming yourself is a form of denying because it is not allowing the reality to exist without qualification or judgment. Even if you can identify a legitimate explanation for the realities: "If he would have done that," or "If she had done this, then I would never have done what I did," or, " ...it never would have happened." It might be true, but by continuing to justify, explain, defend, or hide them, or by laying off blame, or by beating yourself (even if you only do so quietly to yourself), you still are giving additional credence and, therefore, strength, to the denied reality. The only way to lessen the strength and hold a denied reality has on you is to stop denying it. Instead, own it! It's the quickest way to get past it.

NOTE: Our tendency to not own our denied realities comes from the conscious or subconscious belief that if we admit to, and own, our denied realities, and if we do not suppress, defend, or justify them, then our value is at risk.

Owning Your Denied Realities

Owning your denied realities is not the same as blaming and beating yourself for them, judging yourself because of them, liking them, being proud of them, not trying to improve them, not trying to change them, not caring if they happen again, not striving to make sure they don't happen again, or not being sorry they occurred. Owning is acknowledging that a denied reality occurred or exists—irrespective of why or how it happened, whose fault it was, who will know about it, or what will happen next.

Owning a denied reality completely recognizes it as a given. By doing this, no more effort will be expended on justifying it, wishing to change it, trying to change it, or hiding what already happened or what already exists. Denying ownership stokes those denied realities with negative energy, making their impact and their ability to haunt you much stronger. Denying a denied reality is like denying you have cancer. Left unchecked, the cancer continues to grow. Eventually, it overwhelms. It is only when you finally accept the cancer as reality, that you can begin to face it, understand it, cope with it, treat it, reduce it, or even beat it.

Denied realities are part of being human. Your objective as a human being should not be to never make errors, never make decisions you regret, never have flaws, failures, or experiences you don't like, or divest yourself of them. Remember, the goal is not perfection. The goal should be to own these denied realities, regardless of what occurred or why. You need to own them because only then do you strip them of their power. Only then do you give yourself strength over them. Only then can you fully learn and grow from them and focus on your future. That is always your goal.

You may have to provide explanation, apology, or defense in response to legal proceedings, company policy, or an ethics inquiry. You may have to provide a courteous or owed response to someone you hurt. However, that is where explanation and justification should end. Beyond that, it is simply unproductive, unnecessary, and undeserved.

Remember, all of these denied realities are events with beginnings and ends, so it is only after you recognize them as being separate from any absolute significance and from your value, that you can fully allow them, and therefore allow them to sail on by. You do that by owning them.

Again, keep in mind, there's a key difference between disowning, lying about, fighting, defending, or justifying denied realities and owning them. Disowning, fighting, defending and justifying them takes focus, time, effort, and energy to come up with answers or arguments and respond to them. They also don't go away. Owning them takes none of that. Remember, your value is absolute and maintains regardless of any error, flaw, decision, failure, or experience, so the question is not: "How do I undo, defend, disown, fight, justify, or hide something that has occurred, or that I screwed up?" Instead, since it did, indeed, occur, the question is, "What will I do going forward to reach my goal?"

This is true of the most devastating realities as well.

Consider a surgeon who makes a critical error in surgery and his patient dies. He is genuinely sorry, pays for the mistake, and takes steps to ensure it does not happen again. That may be necessary and appropriate, but continually beating, or defending himself because it happened is not, and it helps no one.

As long as the surgeon is compelled to defend, hide, disavow, overcome, beat himself up, justify, or explain his error, he won't get past it, particularly because he was at fault. Remember, performing all these denying acts is difficult work. It takes a great deal of time, focus, and energy. They also cement the reality to you. Owning them takes no time and no energy, and it releases the hold the denied reality has on you.

Now, in the case of the surgeon, he will likely have to answer for the mistake—as he should—and defend himself to a medical board or a court of law. Perhaps he needs to train more, change fields, or even go to prison. But he should not continually beat himself up or be expected to do so because that will reduce his ability to move on, grow, or improve himself. It will not lead to a productive, satisfying life. While seeing the surgeon suffer with guilt for the rest of his life may be the wishes of the family of the dead patient, in reality, self-beating doesn't help the victim, his/her family, or anyone else. When the surgeon owns the reality, he will be able to let it go, move on, and rebuild.

Owning does not release the person from responsibility. It releases the person from self-beating and being stuck—unable to act, to adjust, to grow, to respond absolutely and objectively, and to move on. That is my goal for you when you find yourself in a situation where you are beating yourself, or when someone else is beating you because of something you did.

To sum it all up, take ownership of your errors, flaws, bad experiences, regrettable decisions, and failures. Beyond legal, policy, ethics, general courtesy, or civil obligation, do not continue to explain them or defend them—even to yourself or even when you feel you have a great reason to do so. Do not hide them. Do not continue to justify them. Just own them. Remember, justifying, lying, hiding, and defending errors, flaws, decisions, and failures, and struggling with things you've experienced, provides them with energy. They also increase your focus on the past. This does the opposite of what you want to have happen.

You want to own and leave the denied realities behind you. It may sound backward, but when you deny them, you energize them. You are increasing your focus on them and the hold they have on you. If you don't leave them behind, you cement them to you. You, therefore, are continually forcing yourself to focus on things you no longer have any control over. Once you own the denied realities, you can let them go and focus on your future.

Definitive statements of ownership like "I made the error" period! or "I made a decision I regret" period! or "I failed" period! or "I am flawed" period! or "This happened to me" period! "Now what will I do to go forward?" period! This will take you far. These statements release you from the denied reality. Owning them strips them of their power, gives them finality, and stops the process of ruminating on them.

Don't add *because* or *but* because they are forms of denying, justifying, hiding, or defending it.

- "I failed because …"
- "I forgot the meeting because …"
- "I screwed up because …"
- "I did it, but …"
- "I made the mistake, but …"

It doesn't matter if it was an error, a wrong decision, a flaw, or an actual failure. Maybe it wasn't. Maybe it was an appropriate response given what you knew then, but it did not work. Whatever the case, it doesn't matter. Just own it! Then leave it.

Tenet 31

In order to deal with an error, flaw, bad decision, failure, or negative experience, own it and accept, unconditionally, that you did it. Use that complete ownership to release yourself from

the event and the past, then to kick off toward your future, and move on.

NOTE: Releasing yourself from an event doesn't mean you forget it. it means to accept the reality of it, but allow yourself to move on—to not obsess on it—to not continually punish yourself with it.

Notes

Chapter 21

Letting Embarrassment
Derail You

(13)

*W*hy does an event that embarrasses have particular potency—even more than other kinds of mistakes? How can an embarrassing moment cause us to obsess on it, hide from it and from those associated with it, and even crumble completely because of it? It is because when we feel embarrassed, in addition to making the error, we perceive the error as spotlighting us as silly, naïve, incompetent, or behaving/performing in a manner that makes us look to be "below our station" (lower class – or at least below theirs). This hits our self-concept need squarely and adds an element of self-consciousness (which relates back to your sense of value) to the already present regret, error, bad decision, negative experience, undesirable flaw, or failure.

Remember, an event is embarrassing only if you connect it to your value or believe others are connecting it to your value and you are measuring your value according to how others feel about you. Remember, events, which include embarrassing events, have no absolute significance. They only have the artificial significance you attribute to them, and they never determine your value.

Your value is not connected to any competency! Would you be embarrassed if something you said made it obvious to others that you knew nothing about quantum physics? Probably not. Why? Because, most likely, you are not connecting your value to that particular competency. My guess is that if you know little to nothing about quantum physics and it is not important to you, then you would have no problem telling someone exactly that.

Focusing on Past Embarrassments

So, why is it easier to recall events that bring back feelings of embarrassment than it is to recall past events that promoted feelings of dignity? The answer lies in their basic view of themselves. People who have positive self-images of themselves, their lives and value (an engaged core), will tend to characterize themselves and their lives according to events that have represented them with dignity. In these cases, potentially embarrassing events represent uncharacteristic glitches that can be laughed off or owned and then released. In those cases, the embarrassments are not connected to their value.

However, people with negative self-images tend to characterize themselves and their lives according to their embarrassments. The embarrassments become proof or strong indications of their ongoing inadequacies and bumbling nature. Here, the embarrassing events are (inaccurately) connected to their value. Ultimately, whether they engage their cores will determine how they characterize themselves and the extent to which embarrassments will torture them. Keep all this in mind and engage your core!

Tenet 32

Embarrassment is the belief that, because of an event (your performance), others are not taking, or will not take you, seriously, or will consider you inept, silly, incompetent, or low class. When you deal with an event that causes you embarrassment,

immediately engage your core and own the event, unconditionally. It is actually far easier to let go of it once you own it, than when you defend, hide it, hide from it, or beat yourself because of it.

Focus on the immediate future and say, "Okay. I screwed this up and this is what I will do to avoid similar events in the future."

Notes

Chapter 22

Letting Worry, Fear, Anxiety and Guilt Control You

(14)

*W*orry can consume you if left unchecked. It can suck the energy out of any of us. It can taint our victories and magnify our failures. Worry can impact our emotions, thoughts, perspectives, and behaviors, driving us to performing debilitating and self-destructive acts. It can chew away at us and create such anxiety that any possible opportunity for growth can be categorically rejected, leaving us all but dead.

Concern is a normal, useful, and important heightened state of vigilance. It is intended to keep us aware, focused, and safe. It can help us rectify a potentially negative situation or conflict. When you feel a lack of control over a negative event that you believe has the potential to do harm or damage, it results in worry. The less control one has, or feels one has, and the greater the assumed, or potential negative impact, the greater the worry. While concern and even worry are normal occurrences, and typically cause minimal disruption, if that worry persists due to lack of situation or conflict resolution, anxiety can set in causing mental, emotional and physical dysfunction.

Getting Sucked into the Cycle of Worry

Worry, as I said, if unchecked, can breed reactive emotions, thoughts and behaviors—anxiety. These reactions breed additional negative emotions, which result in additional worries and additional reactive behaviors. Unless you can break that self-feeding and self-perpetuating cycle, the anxiety can become progressively stronger. It can become a relentless disruptive influence on your life, ultimately paralyzing you or making you ill.

What You Can Do to Reduce Your Anxiety

To reduce your anxiety, it is important to realize a perceived lack of control is fueling it. So, the question to ask regarding any anxiety-provoking situation is; "Where do I have control?" In every situation, there is always something you can control. It may not solve your problem completely or stop something terrible from happening, but it will mobilize you to do something that will move you forward and past the current issue that is causing you the anxiety.

Example: You have a family you need to feed and you are concerned that you are going to be laid off. You are understandably very worried and preoccupied. How will you feed your children and pay the rent? You're not sleeping. You feel out of control, vulnerable, bitter, and maybe even inept because you don't know what to do. You have no control over the layoff. To make things worse, you know the boss doesn't like you much. So, you assume it's out of your hands. All you can do is worry. Without a plan or vision of how to remedy the situation, this worry, unchecked, has risen to a state of chronic anxiety.

However, if you reach down to your basic needs levels, you will find things you can control. In this case you might identify that your primary focus is on the safety (financial) level. "Will I be able to care for my family?" It could be the self-concept level. "Am I competent or deserving enough to care for my family? Do I deserve to keep my job?"

But now it's time to ask some other questions. "What can I do now to gain some level of financial safety and feel better about myself?" "Where can I find some control?" This frees you from getting stuck in the prospect of the inevitable layoff and the accompanying defeatist emotions. It also allows you to focus only on the future.

To gain control, you might look for other job options now (even before you find out if you are going to be laid off). You might improve your work performance. You might ask your boss if you are apt to be laid off (so you can either plan, or relax). You might reduce your personal expenses and start saving. You might learn new job skills. You might check on sources for affordable food and clothing if you are concerned that meeting the very basic needs will be a challenge.

There are also peripheral activities such as networking and exercising that may not immediately resolve your financial problems, but they will energize you and focus you on constructive activities, which will keep you looking forward and working toward your future. This keeps you strong, keeps you from getting stuck in the anxiety mode, and opens opportunities for growth.

Don't say, "I just can't lose my job," "I don't have time to talk about basic needs or other options," or "There's nothing I can do about it." That perspective will most assuredly drain your energy and result in panic, defeatism, reactivity, paralysis, bitterness, frustration, and depression. You may not be able to fix everything immediately, but even small steps open doors—even before you see those doors. Every day that you are stuck in anxiety mode, you are the victim. Every day that you are stuck in the victim role is one more day you don't build toward your future—and it is a lost day.

Worry and Fear

Worry, in its most extreme form, is fear. Fear occurs when you feel significant harm is imminent and you can't (or you don't know how to) make yourself, or someone, or something else safe. We all are vulnerable to fear.

So, what about people who are very secure and rarely doubt

themselves, their safety, or their abilities? It is true, these people know very little of fear. This is typically because they have become adept at maneuvering their focus away from anything that threatens them. Instead, they engage their cores. They implement a very quick cognitive and/or physical response to any threat, which reduces the negative emotional energy. They do not get derailed by it, which puts them back in control—not necessarily control over the threat (the event), but over their response to it, over the perspective they hold regarding it, and over their future. When they don't focus on the threat, but instead, on the response, they do not get beaten down, stuck, or frightened by it. However, if they began to obsess about the threat, or if their track record for avoiding such threats were too often unsuccessful, their confidence might falter.

Those who seem undaunted by threats and fears do not necessarily hold some superior gene that makes them invulnerable to fear, anxiety, or pain. They simply have learned to engage their cores and separate themselves and their value from the fear, anxiety or pain, and the events that spawn those emotions and consider them only as jumping-off points from which to focus on their future.

Those who experience fear, even intensively, are not weaker than those who don't. In fact, there are times when worry and fear are useful and necessary tools for keeping you safe. These are appropriate and understandable responses when you, or someone, or something you care about is, in real danger. It becomes an issue of a disengaged core when your fear comes from defining a potential dreaded outcome as having the power to paralyze you or reduce your value or your potential to ever get back up. When you are at risk of losing your job, it is reasonable to be concerned, or frightened, especially if you have a family to care for.

But if you believe that if you lose your job then you are destined for misery, and that you are somehow less of a person—of less value, and if you can see no way out, or believe you will never find another job, or you have stopped trying to find one, then you know your core has disengaged. This makes it more difficult for you to focus on a solution because, instead, you are focusing on your loss of value and fighting to regain it (assuming you haven't already given up trying). That results in an inability to focus on your future in a constructive, goal-oriented manner.

NOTE: When something worries or scares you, the quicker you engage your core and transform that fear into a future-oriented perspective and well-thought-out action, the more successfully you will avoid the emotional trauma and the resulting anxiety, paralysis, or self-destructive reactions that come from it. An OCEANS assessment can help you.

An OCEANS Assessment example:

Consider this example: Tom was a musician, a pianist. In recent years he found he had become petrified just prior to going on to perform. The worry was incessant and had transformed to all-out fear. It was getting worse. Scared to death that he would forget the notes, he would become emotionally distressed and physically sick. He continually visualized himself going up to the piano, freezing, and not knowing what to play. He felt inept and weak. The pieces he played seemed so long. How could he ever hope to get through even one piece without screwing it up? Tom, upon advice, conducted an OCEANS assessment:

O = When he plays, he is unsure if he can play his pieces correctly. C = He has played it right before and has never forgotten any of it (or perhaps he indeed has forgotten notes before). E = He feels scared and embarrassed that he is so unsure. A = He assumes he will forget how to play his pieces. N = The at-risk need levels are self-concept and safety.

S = As a strategy, he will identify what he can control. He will create memory notes. He will undergo stress-reduction training and focusing exercises. Here, Tom separated and analyzed his experiences. He defined and contained the facts and segmented his assumptions and feelings. Then he shifted his efforts from stewing and worrying to strategizing and acting.

NOTE: Keep in mind, in some cases, the OCEANS assessment may be more complex and lengthy, however, the equation is the same.

Worry and Feelings of Guilt

Let's talk about feelings of guilt. Feeling guilty is not being sorry. Feeling guilty is a self-inflicted (always self-inflicted) emotional self-pounding you take to make you pay for damage to someone or something, you feel you unjustly caused. It is a debilitating emotion that can last a lifetime and can taint every positive aspect of your life.

Guilt, in fact, is a useless emotion. I say useless because it is not constructive. It tends to be destructive because it can paralyze you and result in self-beating, neither of which serves to help you resolve, or get past, the event that is the basis of the guilt. It also does nothing to help the victim of your actions. Let me repeat that: It also does nothing to help the victim of your actions. Guilt raises worrisome issues. "How could I have possibly done that?" "I am a terrible person because I did what I did."

During feelings of guilt, you need to own whatever you did. Look to the future and decide if there is anything you can do to make the situation better. If not, what can you learn from it? Is there anything you can do in the future to be sure it doesn't happen again?

NOTE: No one can make you feel guilty. You only feel guilt when you think you have hurt someone or something unjustly and must continually pay for it.

Tenet 33

When faced with worry, anxiety, fear, or guilt, perform an OCEANS assessment to clearly define and sort through what is worrying you, scaring you, or making you feel guilty. Find what you can control and focus on the future. Don't pound yourself

with the past. Most importantly, when those feelings arise, do something. Do not be paralyzed.

NOTE: If you are feeling guilty because you caused someone pain or injury, you must own it. Look at the issue, decide if you can make amends. If you can't, then focus only on the future.

Notes

Chapter 23

Letting the Things Other People Say and Do Control You

(15)

We can be hurt so badly by the things people do and say. They can shake our confidence, and they can bring out in us emotions ranging from anger to despair. They can distract us from our goals and obligations, and they can draw us away from our principles and priorities.

It can take just a single word from a single person to completely seize control of our mood, priorities, judgment, thoughts, sense of self, and behaviors. Someone walks past you, looks at you, and without provocation and says, "hmph," or perhaps he just shakes his head, or rolls his eyes, leaving you confused, demoralized, hurt, angry or defeated. Why do these people have such power on you? Even if it's someone you don't know and will probably never see again, their words and looks can cut deeply. Even if, as far as you can tell, there was no reason for him to look down on you, it can feel like a hot poker in your back. But why? Shouldn't you be completely unconcerned and unfazed by such insignificant acts against you from people you hardly know? Yes? Yes! Then why do you suffer at their words and looks? It's because your core is not engaged, so their noise gets through. This is the noise of people that, if your core had been engaged, would have been filtered and then tossed aside.

With your core engaged, you recognize that when you come across someone who is acting inappropriately, unfairly, unjustly, even abusively, his, or her behavior is simply meeting his/her needs, even if the behavior does not appear to be effective in doing so. I am not saying you should condone inappropriate behaviors, or just accept and allow them to continue to happen—particularly those which are abusive to you, or are otherwise, dangerous, or illegal. But it is important for you to recognize them for what they are—tools to meet needs. Nothing more, nothing less. When you define them as such, you can more easily understand them. Then you no longer are an emotional victim of them because now you understand what they are—tools they are using to meet their needs. Then, you can respond to them strategically and objectively, and from a perspective of strength, or decide not to respond at all, and simply disallow them.

The man who "hmphed" at you for no reason was meeting his need—possibly to stoke his own ego by putting you down. Perhaps he felt you did or said something or you were just there at the right time for him, so he protected himself by pushing back at you. Who know? Who cares?

NOTE: Remember, never take anything said or done to you personally. You accomplish this by engaging your core.

Tenet 34

Recognize that others' behaviors are simply them trying to meet their foundation needs. Don't personalize them. Try to identify what need the person is trying to meet. If you don't know for sure, just guess. I'm not suggesting you should condone the

inappropriate or unjust behaviors of others. Just understand what you are seeing or experiencing. This insight gives you far more strength and control over how you respond to them—or choose not to respond to them at all.

Notes

Chapter 24

Letting Challenging
Personalities Disrupt You

(16)

*U*nderlying the behaviors identified in the last section as well as others, are the personalities of those with whom you are dealing. Sometimes dealing with the personalities of others around you can be a challenge. Particularly personalities that are disruptive, abrasive, aggravating, humiliating, frustrating, or intimidating. If you are extremely secure and your core is engaged, the personalities around you are less likely to disrupt you, hurt you, aggravate you, or intimidate you. But, if your core is not engaged, and if you are not quite sure of yourself, these personalities (the noise) can have tremendous power over you. They can cut you deeply. But, people's personalities, just like their behaviors, are tools they use to meet their needs. Nothing more. Nothing less. While you do not consciously select your personality, it is a tool that can kick into gear spontaneously and, sometimes at inopportune or inappropriate times.

What is it about people's personalities that can put you on your back? People with problem personalities seldom behave in ways you want them to. Loud, accusatory, all-knowing, nasty, intimidating, demanding, abrasive, passive, whiney, judgmental, or cruel personalities operate according to the individual's own needs, preferred methods, past experiences, personal values, priorities, and lessons taught. Any of these may conflict with yours. They also are very difficult to rein in because they are not consciously applied and they are engrained as a result of years the individual has applied them. Here are two of the most challenging:

All-Knowing and Bullying Personalities

All-knowing and bullying personalities can be terribly disruptive. The all-knowing guy always has to be right. When he's right, he makes sure everyone knows it. When he's wrong, he immediately reworks the facts or picks and chooses certain facts while purposefully leaving others out, in, order to justify his mistake.

This person finds it difficult to let anyone else be right and always has to find some flaw in what others say or do. This individual tends to not give credit to others when they are right, and tends to be overly harsh when they are wrong. What may not be apparent is that these behaviors are the result of this person's own insecurities. Being better than others is necessary to feel good about himself or herself.

This means that no one else can ever win. Even if the other person is right about a certain issue or decision, he says, "Of course I knew that." So the person who was initially pleased with her accomplishment is totally invalidated. All this is an example of the All-Knowing protecting himself. It is the All-Knowing's underlying insecurities that cause him to measure his worth, not only by how often he's right, but by how often others are wrong. He thinks he's just a little smarter or a little better than the rest.

The bully is also an insecure individual who protects himself by pushing others around. The bully is more direct and aggressive than the all-knowing individual. In both cases, their behaviors are tools that meet their safety needs. They devalue others because by treating and believing others are weak, inferior and of less value, they think they are stronger, better, and greater in value, which is how they feel safe.

NOTE: The Bully and the All-Knowing may not be consciously aware of their bullying or all-knowing traits and ways, or the impact their devaluing ways have on other people. The safety need may be kicking in spontaneously, along with their bullying or all-knowing reactions to it.

Responding to Challenging Personalities

To effectively respond to challenging personalities, first, recognize that all challenging personalities are tools people use to protect themselves and meet their needs. Then consciously label these individuals and identify their personalities and behaviors merely as tools at the exact time you are experiencing them. This is critical.

Second, recognize that their personalities come from a combination of personal insecurities, what they've been taught, their values, priorities, and experiences.

Third, recognize that challenging personalities tend to elicit your emotions and not your intellect. When you feel your emotions welling up, catch yourself and respond (internally and externally) intellectually, not emotionally. Once you recognize and acknowledge the personality type and its function, you can much more easily deal with it intellectually and objectively. If you can note, for instance, "Oh, he is a bully, and he's doing this to compensate for his own insecurities." Then you can deal with him by holding him out in front of you, separating him from you and intellectually containing him, and then deal with him objectively.

Fourth, remind yourself that you will seldom be able to convince challenging personalities that they are wrong, or to change their ways. Don't make that your goal. Your goal is to maintain your focus on your own plan, your own path, and your own goals. Keep your conversation and your focus on those.

Fifth, don't react to problem personalities. But, if you feel you have to respond to one, do so by sending a message from a position of strength and independence regarding whatever the person with the problem personality is doing or saying. Your message is that you will not be driven, manipulated, or scared off by any behavior or style. "John, if you want to talk to me, that's fine, but do it with respect. You should at least acknowledge that I made a good point here. If you can't, then perhaps you are just too small or narrow-minded." Then, don't look back for any specific desired response. Remember, you are not likely to get it. Your goal is only to communicate these thoughts to John—not to get John to change. Then there is no dependence on John or what he does or says.

Sixth, refocus on your own plan, path, and goals. Walk away or go back to whatever you were doing. The challenging personalities are irrelevant to you. You have said your piece. It's time to move on.

Tenet 35

Recognize that people with problem personalities are meeting their own misguided needs, and that their personalities, their statements and behaviors are merely tools. Respond if you feel you need to, but do so from a position of strength. Stay focused on your goals—and not on the problem personality in front of you. After you say your piece, don't look back.

Notes

Chapter 25

Letting Societal
Expectations Derail You

(17)

*H*ow do you deal with society's expectations, rules, values, biases, and assumptions? It continually judges you based on what you do, how you look, how much you have, and who you are. Then, it treats you accordingly.

The point here is this: Even if you say, "OK, Gary, fine, I realize my value is absolute and I understand the tenets. It's still hard to exist in this society knowing that I am not considered successful enough, good enough, smart enough, talented enough, clever enough, popular enough, good looking enough, or loved enough. I am bombarded by what society says I should be and what I should want. TV, radio, websites, movies, and social media dictate who and what I am supposed to be. How do I not care about those things? Even if I do not need society's acceptance, I still want it."

I am not suggesting that you should not care about those things, nor do I expect you to not want those things. In fact, I hope you do want some of these things. It's healthy to have a vision, and if your vision meshes with the attributes society feels are important, life can be so much easier and more rewarding. But, the key point here is to take care not to misunderstand what these attributes actually are. These attributes are not true indicators of your value. These attributes are merely tools that you can use to guide you in meeting your goals. Some people have more tools than others. If you lack some of those tools, use others. If you disagree with society's preferences, use your position of dissent to propel you in other directions, fully understanding the potential challenges—and own them. Don't just wallow in the discrepancy.

Society Does Not Define You

Society's definitions of value (what it deems are desirable attributes) are artificial measures of your value and they are those of only a limited segment of society, not the entire society. Realize that any and every segment of society is a special interest group with its own agenda and its own view of what people should be like. No single agenda or view has to be yours. Therefore, if you do not fit a specific segment's particular mold, don't sweat it. Look for another or create your own mold.

The fact is your attributes are tools that you can use, guide and sometimes adjust. They are NOT things that society creates. Society only recognizes some aspect of you, and then gives it a thumbs-up, or thumbs-down. You decide what you want, and you decide how to use or respond to your attributes. You own them. They do not own you. You can influence how attributes that you have no control over (age, family background, racial background, disability) will impact you by how you respond to them. Most importantly, they do not define you. What defines you is what you choose to do with them.

Whether or not you hold the agenda and possess the attributes that some segment of society expects you to have, at the desired level and priority, is not the defining factor that determines your place, future, or value. It is ultimately, and entirely up to you to decide the extent to which you will follow a particular agenda that some part of society has set for you.

You Don't Have to Be Controlled by Society

We can so easily consider ourselves victims or pawns of society. Actually, we are quite capable of creating our own realities. Through our perspectives, assumptions, decisions and actions, we can continually create, recreate, and drive our lives.

If you believe you cannot do, or change something because of some societal influence, you are liable to fail. You may avoid trying altogether. In these cases, inevitably you will rationalize your decisions to do nothing and believe there is a good reason. The reality, however, is that there is no good excuse for passively allowing society, any part of it, or anyone in it, to determine your fate. You will have to concede some battles, but even then, you can still decide how you will respond to such concessions and how you will design your future.

I'm saying, here, that you always have some control over how those things will impact you and, more importantly, how you will respond to them. Don't let even the unchangeable lock you into a position or a future you do not want. There is always something you can change—even if the initial change is small. Find it!

Tenet 36

Societal expectations are real and need to be considered, but only as guides that you consider as you make your decisions and apply your efforts toward your growth and your goals. They are not the determining factors of your identity, plan, future or value. Your future is yours to create—and so is your plan. Remember, your value is a given.

Notes

Chapter 26

Letting Competition Consume You

(18)

*J*ean always compared herself to her older sister who was first in her class. She was smarter, prettier, and everyone's favorite. Jean never felt like she measured up. She was always a sad second.

Nothing can cause more anxiety, depression, insecurity, and bitterness than competing with others who you feel tested or bested by. Assessing your position or value, setting goals and planning your next moves based upon what someone else is doing or what he or she has, or has achieved can cause you to become depressed, distracted, exhausted, bitter, and frustrated. At some point, that will defeat you. It can also cause you to make huge mistakes in judgment.

Consider the runner who is running a race and keeps looking back at his competition. By doing so, he loses his concentration, his stride, his balance, his perspective, and perhaps his confidence if his competition is gaining on him. He loses control or reactively abruptly changes his game plan several times over the course of the race and loses his stride. As he's looking back, he trips and falls. Ultimately, he loses.

Decide who you are and what you want. That should drive you—not what your competition is doing. If you do want what another has, you must determine your own best way to accomplish or attain it. Do not compete against someone who you perceive as having it. This can become a particular challenge when it appears to you that another individual has come by his or her status undeservingly. How do you deal with that? The answer lies in your ability and willingness to step back, allow him/her whatever he/she has, or gets, and look only at your own goals and your own next move—absolutely independent of the other person—on your own terms. How? By engaging your core.

Tenet 37

Compete with no one. Race only against yourself. Focus only on your goals—and not on your competition or the assets they have. Do this by engaging your core.

Notes

Chapter 27

Playing and Replaying Past Life Clips

(19)

When you make a regular practice of reliving negative past experiences over and over again, obsessing about how they went down, or thinking of how things might have been different, you are in danger of getting stuck trying to change your past.

This is like trying to rewrite a letter that has already been sent and read. So, why is it you can be tormented by these negative clips of past life events such as a bad investment, an argument, a breakup, an embarrassing moment, or a missed catch during a baseball game—twenty years ago. Why do you relive these memories over and over again, when you would, most certainly, rather forget them?

Why Negative Life Clips Stay with You

These life clips of negative events become stuck to you when you connect your value to them. You focus on the negative clips because you have come to base your value on negative experiences you have had, instead of positive ones you have had. Those are the clips you continue to run because they are the ones by which you are defining yourself and your life. This practice occurs when your core is not engaged. These clips tend to be heavily weighted, meaning they stand out and they highlight and magnify the bad things that happen to you, and obscure the good things.

Tenet 38

When your core is not engaged, the tendency is to grab onto life clips of negative past events and attach them to your consciousness, and use them to measure your value. Engage your core to cut them loose.

Why You Relive the Negative Ones

Replaying negative life clips can appear to help you in five ways, but they can ultimately harm you greatly.

First, it's a way to protect yourself from harm by seeing if a past negative event still hurts or if you are still vulnerable. But, it will tend to reopen the wound, strengthen the negative impact of the event, and reinforce your belief that you lack value. You then, will tend to put up walls to others and future opportunities to protect yourself, which will keep you trapped in the past.

Second, it's a way to pay for your guilt by punishing yourself by reliving your weaknesses, stupidity, or transgressions. That way it makes you pay for whatever you did wrong, again and again. But, it only gets you stuck focusing on your guilt and your past, which will keep you down and unable to do good. Doing good is how you pay back for a transgression, not by continuing to suffer.

Third, it's a way to protect yourself from future failure by using the past negative life clips to remind you of past failures. Then to remind you to not risk further failure. But, it will keep you from taking chances, and if you don't take chances, you cannot grow.

Fourth, it's a way to protect yourself from feeling weak and inadequate. You create a *martyr moment* by revisiting a negative moment in your life. You feel that weathering a particularly bad time is evidence of your strength, tenacity, and entitlement to respect and good things to come. But, in reality, it keeps you stuck in your past, and it keeps you from growing.

Fifth, it's a habit. Highlighting your negatives is how you always measure your life, your success and your value.

The problem is, whether you are using negative life clips to check your vulnerability, punish yourself, keep yourself safe, extol your virtues, or simply out of habit of weighing your negatives, they keep you connected, even stuck, to those past negative events. It takes a conscious effort not to add to that trend by latching on to a particular past negative life clip. Remember the river? This practice will pull you along until it pulls you under.

Tenet 39

Reliving negative past events (replaying life clips) is a self-protecting device, but actually it does little to protect you. In reality, it reinforces the negative event and your assumptions of having less value. It keeps you stuck there, and it keeps you from focusing on your future. Engage your core—and reach to your future.

Consider this: If you, at some point, were attacked as you walked to your car, it would be understandable that you would be on watch every second, at least for a period of time. It would also be understandable if you'd keep thinking back to that day. The intent is to be sure it never happens again. But to continually focus on what already occurred will do you no good—no matter how many times you replay that clip. Recalling a negative past event should only be done briefly, but then you have to shift your focus and your energy to identifying a strategy for ensuring a safer future.

When Even the Good Goes Bad

You get home after a party. Everyone was happy and friendly. You had a great time. You spoke to everyone. You were entertaining and pleasantly distracted from the trials of your daily life. You were comfortable and relaxed. It was a perfect evening.

You sit down, watch TV, and go to bed. At three in the morning, you are awakened by a nondescript internal gnawing. Then it begins. You begin to play back the entire party, moment by moment. You can't identify one specific thing—there's not even a specific clip to play—but you feel that something painted you in a bad light. You begin the process of reliving each event that took place at the party—every interaction. Finally, your mind hits upon one incident. You were talking about something insignificant with two others and answered a single question in a way you felt made you look a little stupid. That is the clip you now replay over and over.

Why were you compelled to search and search and search until you finally found something negative? If you have a basic underlying belief or assumption (even subconsciously) that you are not of value, not capable, not competent, not deserving of good things, or that your life is just cursed, then you will tend to focus on the bad. You will be less likely to believe the good things that have happened to you are, in fact, good. You will define yourself as good, if and only if, you can find no negative event. So, you search. Inevitably you will find a negative event (because we all have them), or you create one because you know they are always there somewhere. But, in any case, you will determine that because you were able to identify a negative in your past, you have proven you are, in some way, substandard.

If you have experienced negative moments, the experiences can haunt you for years. This haunting can transform into expectation of similar future negative events. The expectations can become so strong that you fall into a pattern of sabotaging yourself, resulting in more negative events.

NOTE: Allow yourself to enjoy the victories of your day. Don't let the negative perception of one event paint the entire day as bad. There is always some aspect of every day that is good. Find it! Say it out loud. Write it down. If you are saying, "I don't seek out the bad." Maybe so, but are you sure? Check it out.

Searching for negatives is an ironic attempt to protect yourself and feel better by getting in touch with something that hurt you—a negative event. This is intended to put yourself into a position where you can effectively cope with your life or at least explain it. But, when you do this, your interpretation, judgment and explanation can be laced with emotionally flawed assumptions and absurd generalities that support the contention that you are dysfunctional or substandard.

Tenet 40

Focusing on the negatives, in reality, gets you stuck on some of the most painful moments of your life. You need to seek protection, comfort, strength, and your role in life by looking at the future. Let the past go. When the negative event creeps in, own it! It happened. It started. It ended. Now move on. The more you own a past negative event (not relive it), the less pull it will have on you, and the need to search it out and relive it will be gone.

Past Glories

We don't always have to think back on bad times to get stuck. We can get stuck on past good times as well. Thinking back on good times, successes, and glories can be a positive practice if you get strength, joy, hope, confidence, and energy from them to propel you to new good times, successes, and glories. In fact, this is a sign of an engaged core. However, if you keep thinking back to your past glories, but you see them only as good times long since past—never to be experienced again—they can become shackles that will keep you imprisoned in the past. You will be unable to find, recognize, and enjoy new positive experiences.

If you rather sadly think of the big game back in high school where you made the winning catch twenty years ago as the best day of your life and a primary indicator of your value, it is an example of defining your value by past glories. In cases such as this, you keep looking back to past glories, successes, or fabulous times and assuming, asserting, and lamenting that nothing will ever compare to them. Past glories should be celebrated as enduring successes that propel you toward your future. Don't turn them into haunting memories that serve as the roots of your imprisonment in the past. If the primary measure of your life is in the past, your future will never measure up.

Notes

Chapter 28

Giving Away Your Power

(20)

You can actually give away the power you have to create options, and control your responses, your future and your growth. You do this by reacting (acting impulsively and emotionally) instead of responding (acting thoughtfully, objectively and with wisdom) This occurs in three ways, particularly when you are emotionally charged, by impulsively:

Conceding. Withdrawing or isolating from, giving up on, or giving in to negative events or situations.

Attacking outwardly. Directly or indirectly, physically or verbally, trying to hurt whatever is negatively impacting you during or after a negative event or situation.

Attacking inwardly. Beating yourself, becoming anxious, or depressed. Turning on yourself for being negatively impacted by, causing, or not being able to fix the negative event, or for being weak, or inept.

Let me give you some examples to drive this concept home:

Example 1: Your neighbor constantly makes too much noise during late-night parties. So you become reactive and give away your power impulsively by...

Conceding. You decide it's no use, so you just endure it, you move away, or you put up a big fence.

Attacking outwardly. You hit him or sue him.

Attacking inwardly. You become frustrated, anxious, or insulted. You stew about it or become angry at yourself for not doing more, or depressed because you feel powerless.

Example 2: You have a fight with your spouse about the fact that your spouse bought a car without telling you. You react impulsively by ...

Conceding. You say, "Do whatever the hell you want."

Attacking outwardly. You scream and throw things or ask for a divorce.

Attacking inwardly. You blame yourself for not being able to resolve the situation or control your spouse. You become depressed or you seethe inside.

Keeping Your Power

In order to deal most effectively with a negative event, you have to ask yourself, "What can I do that will most likely not cause additional harm to the situation, to others, or to me. What will best meet my short-term objective? What will best meet my long-term goals?" This is the process of responding as opposed to reacting.

Responding does not involve any of the options identified in the two examples above. Responding includes the following steps:

1. Identify the problem clearly.
2. Check for the presence of emotions and ego rushes and put them in check.
3. Separate absolute significance statements from impact statements and deal only with the impact statements.
4. Identify your short-term objectives.
5. Identify your long-term goals.
6. Identify your options.
7. Identify potential immediate, short-term, and long-term damage to your short-term objectives and long-term goals.
8. Select the option that does the least harm and best meets your short-term objectives and long-term goals.
9. Ask yourself, if the option that you selected is not only right, but wise.

NOTE: Sometimes one goal or objective must suffer in order to better meet one that is more important or more immediate. This is where wisdom comes in—where you must ask if wisdom suggests that you should focus on one goal or objective and not on the other. What is the relative risk and potential outcome of each?

Tenet 41

Make sure you are responding and not reacting. This way, you can make sure you do not give away your power by making rash or damaging decisions. The ability to respond—and not react—is a sign of an engaged core.

Notes

Chapter 29

Ignoring Your Options

(21)

*I*t is important to recognize that there is the opportunity for some kind of choice in some aspect of every event. From whether to go left or right, to which job to take, to how you are going to respond when faced with a major threat, conflict, or challenge, to how you will deal with inevitable grief or loss. Recognizing you always have choices, and understanding that life is, at its most basic level, a series of choices, allows you to realize the freedom you seek. The freedom you have. This is imperative. If you fail to see the choice component of an event that is taking place in your life, you become powerless—a slave to it. When you become powerless, you become a victim of it, resulting in frustration, anger, fear, depression, paralysis, and ultimately defeat.

The more you engage your core, the more you can see your choices. Keep in mind that having two choices is no more than an ultimatum. Always look for the third choice. The third choice gives you freedom and control.

Here is an example of an issue that Fred is facing, and his three choices: "If I can't be with Mary, I don't want to live." Choice 1: Being with Mary. Choice 2: Not living (the ultimatum). Choice 3: Focus on new relationships. "I can't be with Mary but I am not ready to take my life. So instead, even though I can't imagine finding someone else as wonderful as Mary, I will develop new relationships" (meeting new people, etc.) The third choice gives him freedom.

Tenet 42

There are always options, but remember, two options constitute an ultimatum. Don't stop looking until you find at least three. The third one (though, in some cases, you may not like that one much, either) will free you every time. Look for it.

Notes

Chapter 30

Standing on a Particular Principle or Personal Standard

(22)

What about principle? Aren't having principles a good thing? Haven't we always been taught to have them and to stand by them? Yes. However, standing on principle at the expense of wisdom can disempower us by shackling us to decisions that can cause great harm to us and to others if either, two principles are competing with each other or if they are not considered and applied with wisdom.

Example: Since she was a young girl, Sue maintained the principle that she should always respect her father. To her, it meant she should always please him. Her father always said he wanted her to work in the family business, a clothing store, so that's what she did. But Sue was miserable. She never wanted to work there, and at the age of fifty-three, she found herself depressed. The principle of pleasing her father at all costs became a problem because it conflicted with another principle she held: that she should help people who are suffering. Sue wanted to be a doctor. Here, two principles conflicted with each other.

In this next example, wisdom was not applied and the result was pain. Your principle states you should always be honest. You tell Jean, a friend of yours, that she is gaining too much weight. The problem is that Jean is already struggling with depression, and this puts her over the edge. She tries to kill herself. The question, here is, was it necessary or wise to tell the truth? Or would it have been wiser to withhold the truth to spare Jean's feelings? That is a personal decision and its potential impact needed to be considered carefully. In this case, the principle of honesty versus the wisdom of adhering to that principle had to be considered. Which one should be adhered to? That's your call, but it's a call that has to be made carefully.

Do not get stuck adhering to a particular principle if wisdom tells you something's wrong in doing so. Look closely at the varying areas of impact. Look deep. Perhaps if Jean had been on the verge of dying due to obesity, the priority would be to be honest and tell her she weighed too much. But if her physical health related to obesity had not been an immediate issue, perhaps her feelings should have taken precedence. Either way, you decide.

There is one more potential problem. This is where you stand on a principle because you are scared to step out.

Example; Max believed he should always prepare for the future. This is what he was always taught by his father. So he never spent any money. He only saved it in case of emergency. Therefore, he never went anywhere, did anything, or bought anything just for the fun of it. He always lived in near squalor—even though he had the money with which he could have enjoyed his life. He lived a very sheltered, sad, and miserable life, and died wealthy, empty, and scared—all due to the fact he was scared to spend his hard-earned cash due to a questionable principle.

Tenet 43

Do not get stuck adhering to one principle if wisdom tells you something's wrong or if it results in you being miserable. When two conflicting principles are at play, infusing wisdom will help you to select the one which will minimize harm and maximize

positive growth. Do not get stuck because you're scared to try something new. Ask yourself why you are standing on this principle, and look at its short-term and long-term impact. Do not let any principle force you into a life of misery or emptiness. That is not their purpose. Their purpose is to spur you on to a meaningful and rewarding existence according to your values and ethical standards. But life is not black and white. There are many nuances and variables we deal with every single day. So be sure to infuse wisdom when adhering to or selecting the most appropriate principle.

Notes

Chapter 31

Self-Defeating Behaviors and Their Opposing Forces

(23)

*M*any of us have looked back on something someone has done, and said, "Why did he do that? It just made things worse," "She knew better, but she did it anyway … Why?" or "Why does he always do that?" Or perhaps others have said those things about us, or perhaps we've said it about ourselves. These behaviors are often labeled as self-defeating, and they can strip us of our power to find our place. In some cases, one self-defeating behavior (SDB) can lead us to another and another and another and another. Why do we, sometimes, seem to be on this path of self-destruction? Actually, self-defeating behaviors are not so mysterious when you consider the fact that the term is a misnomer. In reality, a self-defeating behavior is an action that is assumed (by others, or ourselves) to be intended to achieve a particular goal, but (perhaps unconsciously) it is intended to meet another more immediate goal.

It may create a barrier to achieving the assumed intended goal or it may achieve the intended goal, but cause other problems. Sometimes the intended goal is assumed to be such by others, but it is not the intended goal of the person performing them at all. In any case, it is not self-defeating. It ultimately does achieve the intended goal at the moment. I know, it's a little confusing. Consider this example:

An employee asks for a raise, but he does so in a demanding, angry fashion, thereby angering the boss and not getting the raise. Self-defeating? Yes, if the goal was to get the raise. But in reality, in this case, the more immediate and stronger goal (perhaps sub-consciously), was letting his boss know he was angry. It was not to get the raise. So was the behavior self-defeating? No, the man was successful in communicating his anger—the true intended goal. Be careful. Make sure you know what your goal is and be sure that your actions will support it. This is important, but complex, so please read this section several times until it is crystal clear.

One final consideration is that SDBs also bring with them assumptions. In this case, the assumption was that letting the boss know how angry he was would result in the boss granting the raise. In this case, the raise was the goal, but the assumption of the best path was flawed. But, even so, the immediate goal (or intent) was to let the boss know how upset he was—and he succeeded.

The Presence of Opposing Forces

The concept of opposing forces explains how those self-defeating behaviors occur. It explains that for every decision you have to make, there are multiple perspectives and priorities that are waiting in the wings, ready to lead you to potentially make different decisions. Each perspective and resulting decision meets a different goal (or the same goal in a different way). Further, every goal relates back to one of the basic needs levels.

In the majority of cases, one perspective on an issue is significantly stronger than the others. So, acting on this perspective (making the decision) is simple, and the opposing forces may even go completely unnoticed. Consider, in the morning when you want some jam for your toast, you reach for the jam jar and not the butter, or the broom. A simple decision. However, in some cases you find yourself torn about which goal to focus on, or how. The decision you ultimately make may appear to some as self-defeating, but if you are aware of the opposing forces at play, and why, you will see how the behavior did, in fact, reach the intended goal and one of the need levels.

There are many examples of opposing forces at play that are seen as self-defeating behaviors, but in actuality, are achieving the intended goals. Consider these:

The Dieter

Dan is on a diet. He eats very carefully, making sure that his diet is low in fat and healthy. He goes to a restaurant and eats all the right things. When the server asks if he would like dessert, Dan struggles. "Should I—or shouldn't I?" Here, there are two perspectives (forces) fighting for position, and each perspective responds to a different goal that relates back to a basic need. "I should not eat the dessert because I want to be healthy and lose weight" (safety need level). "I should eat the dessert because I've had a tough week, and I deserve to do something nice for me" (self-concept need level). If he eats the dessert, it meets a goal. Those who know he wants to lose weight will likely see the behavior as an SDB. The opposing forces at play were eating or not eating the dessert.

The Rickety Ladder

Tom climbs a ladder. He knows is rickety. He climbs it and its rungs split and he falls because he is in a hurry to get the job done and there is no other ladder close by. He's always in a hurry. It makes him feel good to do things quickly because then he can look back and see how much he's accomplished and how capable he is. Here, the goal/need to be safe (safety level) is less strong than the goal/need of accomplishment and speed (self-concept level). His perspective is that it's worth the risk (or he under-estimates the risk), and he makes a decision that does not consider his safety (which is likely to appear to others as self-defeating). The opposing forces at play were climbing or not climbing the ladder.

The Competence-Seeker

Sarah's goal is to be considered competent at work. But instead of modeling competence by being creative, efficient and helpful to coworkers by sharing her insights while considering others' feelings, she attempts to demonstrate her competency by boasting, shoving her ideas down others' throats, and criticizing others' ideas. The result is that while others agree she's smart, no one can stand her. The path she chose towards perceived competency was different than the path we might have chosen.

We might assume she would use positive support, guidance, and solid leadership skills to demonstrate her competence. But Instead she uses aggressiveness to try to get people to see her competence because she believes that it is the clearest and most efficient way to get them to see how much she knows. Self-defeating? No. She succeeded in letting everyone know how much she knows, but it damaged her reputation and employee morale. The opposing forces at play were providing positive support and being aggressive (both of which were intended to meet self-concept level needs in different ways).

Young Love

Bob is in high school and likes Sandy. He approaches her and asks her out, but she says no. His perspective is that if he keeps asking her out, she will see how serious he is and how much he likes her, and she will ultimately say yes. So, he keeps asking her with more and more pressure until he thoroughly alienates her.

He kept pushing and pushing until there was no chance of reaching his goal of having Sandy go out with him. Instead, he pushed her away. Sandy did find out how much he liked her, but she wanted no part of him. The self-defeating behavior was the persistent asking.

The opposing forces at play were continuing asking versus giving her space. The behavior responded to his perception that she didn't realize how much he liked her, and telling her again and again made sure she did. He succeeded in communicating how much he liked her, but not achieve his original goal of getting her to like him.

These are all examples of SDBs and opposing forces, and the goals and needs they were intended to meet; and their functionality.

NOTE: If we examine our own behaviors closely enough, we might find that we are meeting a need or goal other than the one we think we are trying to meet. When things are going wrong, take a closer look at what you're doing, and why. Consider other paths.

Walking into the Chopper Blade with Your Eyes Wide Open

In some situations, like the ones above, you may not be consciously aware that your behavior is self-defeating. When your focus on the immediate event and your immediate needs is particularly strong, it can impede your ability to see the larger issues and how they might impact you down the road.

In other situations, however, you can actually create a self-defeating negative situation fully aware of the fact that you will regret it later. The question is, why would you put yourself in that position? In these cases, principles and your own priorities at the moment take precedence over wisdom and longer term impact. In these cases, your priority might be to:

- Release extreme levels of energy. "I was getting so angry I just had to throw the paperweight through the window. I didn't care that I was going to smash it and then have to pay for it.
- Assert yourself to make a point and/or maintain self-respect. You bolt out of the office, stating you're quitting after a disagreement with your boss—even though you know you will be unable to pay your bills.

- Keep yourself, or something or someone you care about, safe by sabotaging an existing plan. "I've got to stop this now. So, I'm going to the newspapers—even though it's against policy and I will likely get fired."
- Payback/punish. You shoot your wife's lover because you don't care about the long-term impact on your life (prison).

In all these cases, while you may regret them as soon as the outcome is upon you, they did meet specific immediate goals and basic needs at that moment. There can also be a tacit assumption that the negative outcome, while objectively speaking, is inevitable, will not or may not happen.

NOTE: Acting in a manner that serves your purpose now at the expense of future safety may be wise and appropriate. You may have a large very important report due tomorrow, but instead of working on it, you spend the evening with a friend who just lost her mother. You lose your job because of it. Self-defeating? Your call.

Tenet 44

A self-defeating behavior is an action that is assumed to be intended to achieve a particular goal, but (perhaps unconsciously) it meets another more immediate goal. It may actually create a larger barrier to achieving the assumed intended goal, or it may achieve the assumed intended goal, but cause other problems in other areas.

It is up to you to recognize your own SDB and the opposing forces at play. You must determine what need it is meeting and how it is meeting it. If it isn't working—or if it is but it is also causing other problems—find another behavior that will be more effective in the short term, as well as the long term. Separate your decision from all emotion. Don't give in to the short-term reactive fixes, even if they are, in some way, absolutely justified unless

you've thoroughly evaluated all aspects of the potential impact—both short-term and long-term. This process can be helpful for understanding and responding to others' SDBs as well, thereby reducing the chances that you will be hurt by it down the road. All this will help you find your place.

Old Habits

This is a good time to talk about your habits. People say, "It's just a bad habit I have." How many times have I heard (and said) that? A habit is nothing more than an overused path of behavior—often a SDB. A path that is intended to achieve a goal and meet a need. It's a path that has become comfortable, safe, easy, spontaneous, or without thought or planning (at least compared to other behavioral options). A bad habit is a path that, most likely, at some time in the past, in some instance, was effective, but is now, in some way, causing you trouble. To break a bad habit, you have to blaze a new path. To do this, identify the habit that is causing you distress. Identify the goal and the basic need the habit is intended to meet. Identify the resulting problem it causes. Then identify the goal and need it is actually meeting (it will be different). Then, look for another way to meet that same goal that will not cause the same (or different) problems. Or at least will cause fewer, or less severe problems.

Example: Jim had a habit of being five or ten minutes late for everything. Friends and colleagues had come to expect it. When asked about it, Jim would say, "Something always seems to come up at the last minute." It was a bad habit. The reality is that his constantly being late met a need at some point in his life. When Jim was younger, he always felt uncomfortable when dealing with other people. Being late helped him feel a sense of control over an uncomfortable situation by coming into it on his own terms and minimizing the length of time he would have to interact with others. While it served that need well, it now has become a bad habit because now he is always late for everything and is likely to lose his job due to his constant tardiness.

NOTE: Consider your habits. Ask yourself why do you smoke,

overeat, gamble, drink, overreact, bite your nails, or overspend? What goal does it achieve? What need does it meet? How does it hurt you? How else can you achieve your goal and meet the need without being hurt—at least so badly by it?

Eliminating a habit is difficult. But it can be done. Identify an alternative—even if it isn't quite as satisfying as the bad habit—and use it. Keep at it—especially when you really don't want to.

Notes

Chapter 32

Not Confronting Negative Events

(24)

*W*e have all felt victimized by negative events and have experienced at least a moment of emotional paralysis as a result. In severe cases, the inability to respond positively can last a lifetime and leave you beaten, scarred, scared, and directionless as you wander through life. Remember the man who lost his wife 20 years before.

Paralysis is a mechanism that actually is intended to keep you from further harm. But, after a particular negative event, if you protect yourself from it by inaction instead of protecting yourself through positive action, it will keep you from engaging your core and overcoming the distress. You can end up permanently mired in the devastating, immoveable shadow of that negative event.

Except in certain situations of potential physical harm, inaction is typically not the best action to take. When in physical peril, paralysis tries to shut down, conserve energy, reduce demand, or hide the body in order to protect it from further physical harm. However, when in emotional peril, this shutting down, too often, perpetuates the problem and the emotional pain or stifles the emotional pain that eventually explodes inside of you. By moving, creating, and accomplishing, you generate ideas, options, plans, and cognitive, physical, and positive emotional energy. You ultimately identify and implement a new event that has the potential to improve the situation.

Illustration: If you get caught standing in the rain, you have the option of staying there until the rain stops, all the while, getting soaked, or you walking toward the closest shelter to get dry. Standing in the rain will not help your situation, but walking toward a shelter gets you closer to getting dry.

Paralysis can disguise itself as a justifiable response. "There's nothing I can do." "Nothing I do works out anyway." "Why should I be the one to change?" "I don't want to make things worse." Or, "I don't know what to do." "I'm afraid to try anything." "I just need to rest and think for a while." Fair enough. But you have to move beyond that. The question to ask is, will doing nothing improve your situation? Will it help you meet your need and achieve your goal? Will it put you in a better position and make you happier now, tomorrow, next week, next month, or next year?

Sometimes, it can look and feel like inaction is the best action to take against further harm, or against being targeted. In reality, inaction tends to make you a bigger target, and it puts you at risk of greater harm. It can keep you stuck in a victim's role. If you do decide to hold tight, be sure you can explain how this will get you where you want to go. If you can't, then reconsider.

NOTE: Keep in mind, action does not mean reckless or obsessive reactiveness. It means wise, strategic, thoughtful, measured response.

Tenet 45

Don't become emotionally paralyzed. Think, plan, and respond—but do so strategically and not rashly, reactively or vindictively. If you choose not acting as your strategic response, be sure it will really take you where you want to go.

Notes

Chapter 33

Reverting to Old Roles

(25)

*H*ave you ever found yourself in a situation where you were surrounded by people, places, or activities that seem to pull you back to past times, places, or situations where you filled a very different role than the one you fill today? Then, experiencing all the feelings, reactions, insecurities, resentments, frustrations, and lack of power you experienced then? It might occur when you spend time with family or friends who knew you when you were younger, less experienced, and less stable or when you made poor choices. You may revert to that role when someone or something not directly associated with your past, triggers that role.

Regardless of your age or current role, being relegated to an old role can frustrate and destabilize you. It can damage your self-esteem and shake your confidence. You can find yourself questioning if you have, indeed, progressed from the old days at all. You can find yourself resenting the person who is pulling you back. Resenting that he/she cannot, or will not recognize that you have, indeed, grown and evolved. It also can result in your making poor new decisions in reaction to being put into this old role. These feelings can come from others who treat you like a kid or a novice in your field. Sometimes, it's all internal and you do it to yourself when you assume that others see you a certain way or when you are questioning your own competence. It can remind you of times when you were less knowledgeable, less experienced, or less competent, and then you end up feeling like you have not progressed at all.

When you feel such a past role relegation triggered, you need to, first, recognize it. Once you recognize the role you are being pulled into, you need to assert to yourself, your current role, abilities, and accomplishments. Further, and most importantly, you need to remember you are not there to prove to anyone else that you now fill a different role. Just respond to whatever you encounter from the perspective of your current role, not from any past, or different role in which someone, or something else is trying to put you. Do so without emotion or defensiveness.

Example: Here are two responses (old role versus new role) to your mother who is criticizing you for the apartment you are living in because she feels it's not good enough

Old role response. "Mother, I'm twenty-seven years old. I'm capable of deciding where I'm going to live. I'm not a kid anymore. Besides, I like it there, and it's really none of your business. You aren't the one who is living there. When are you going to stop treating me like a kid?"

New role response. "I understand you don't like me living there because you think it's not good enough, and I appreciate that. But, I like the apartment and the neighborhood, and it is located near my work. I don't have to drive every day, so I save on gas. I probably won't live there forever, but for now, I really like it. I do appreciate your concern, but let's talk about something else"

Tenet 46

Remember, old undesirable roles can creep back into your life. Don't be drawn into filling them. Respond to role regulation from your current role—and not from the old one that is long gone.

Note

Chapter 34

Procrastinating

(26)

*Y*ou have a report due in two months. You know what needs to be done and you know how to do it. You absolutely do not want to be scrambling to get it done at the last minute. So you sit down to do it, but then you stop. The night before it is due, you still haven't done it, and you are doing the very scrambling you swore you would not do. Why?

Procrastination can be a maddening and even a devastating occurrence. Lives have been wasted, jobs have been lost, marriages have been destroyed, classes have been failed, and anxiety has been raised to unbearable levels as a result of just not getting to it, whatever it is. So what exactly is procrastination? Procrastination is a vehicle intended to meet an immediate need via a quick fix, at the expense of more important, more significant, larger, or longer-term needs and goals. The control and power we hold is quickly lost due to procrastinating.

While it may not seem like it, procrastination is like any other behavior. It is a tool that serves a specific purpose. The purpose, as we have said before, is to meet one of our basic needs. But, the need it is meeting is immediate and the strongest at the moment, but it disregards entirely, a more important, or significant need that requires attention now. It will soon become more immediate and more critical.

Let's look more closely at the example above. You put aside the time to do the report. You have all the materials. You're staring at them, but when you think about doing the report, you start to feel uneasy. You feel you have to get away from it for a while. Maybe you feel fatigue setting in and need to rest. Maybe you start to rationalize that you still have time or that if you don't get it done, you can deal comfortably with the repercussions. You might decide to work on other things that are less pressing because you figure if you get those things done and out of the way, you will be able to better concentrate on the hard stuff later. You may turn to physical, concrete, or maintenance kinds of activities that are easier or faster to get done, because you'll feel like you really accomplished something. Maybe you turn on a movie or go out with friends because you deserve it. The possibilities are endless.

Whatever you decide to do instead of doing the report, (this is the act of procrastinating). The procrastination is not necessarily a lack of insights about the potential fallout or the importance of the activity you are delaying working on. What is it then? Procrastination is a SDB—a tool that meets the most immediate need at that moment. The problem is that it meets an immediate (but not necessarily the most important or most significant) need, and it typically meets it with quick fixes, and in limited, short-sighted ways, at the expense of wisdom and longer-term, more significant, and more important goals and needs. Most importantly, it has little regard for the future negative repercussions.

Look at this example: John kept putting off going to the doctor to have the pain in his stomach checked out. Eventually he did go in when the pain became unbearable, only to find that he had major intestinal damage that required surgery. Instead of looking ahead at the possible severe repercussions resulting from not getting proper care early, he only looked at his immediate needs (safety – he felt safer not knowing) and kept taking antacids. Besides, the short-term fix was cheaper (financial safety), and he did not have to miss any work (financial safety). Plus, he hated going to the doctor for anything.

To better understand procrastination, go back to your basic needs and recall the concepts of SDBs and opposing forces. There are always several at play.

NOTE: The toughest thing about avoiding procrastination is starting a task. Once you start, you are far more likely to stay on task.

Tenet 47

Procrastination is a vehicle intended to meet an immediate need via a quick fix, at the expense of more important, more significant, larger, or longer-term needs, goals and implications. When faced with the potential that you might procrastinate, focus on the potential longer-term negative impact that will result from procrastinating and visualize the impact in detail and the feelings you will have if you don't get it done now. Then, plan the completion of the activity the night before you are to start it. Visualize it in detail. Then agree to just start it.

When you do so, if it can't be practically and realistically completed right away—or you are just compelled to do something else—select an amount of work from the task at hand you will complete at that sitting. Go a small distance (five minutes or one or two steps) beyond where you thought you would originally stop. This will mobilize and energize you without overwhelming you. Then plan your next effort toward completion.

By continually selecting a goal for each sitting, then progressing just a few steps further, it will stretch your ability to address the task while not putting such great pressure on you to the point where even thinking about it, causes you to put it off. It will put you back in the driver's seat—not being directed by the forces of procrastination. It will also result in your getting at least a little more done. If you agree to do five more minutes than the plan stated, do the five and then two more.

Notes

Chapter 35

Skipping Steps – Losing the Logic Piece

(27)

*I*t is all too easy to skip steps when times get tough or you are rushed. You can jump ahead, not do your homework, not cover all the bases, not communicate fully, not consider all the contingencies of possible outcomes, not complete your duties, or not double-check the facts or your work. In those cases, the result can be disastrous.

When building a bridge, missing a few bolts and rivets in the interest of saving time and money can be devastating. The time and effort saved provides only limited, short-term benefits and often causes severe damage down the line. Skipping steps is the primary reason the logic in what we do is lost. When you perform illogically, things go wrong.

Test it out. Consider an event in your life that went wrong. Go through the steps you took prior to, during, and after it. Can you identify any step that was missed or something you might have done differently that would have improved the result? If so, that missing, or wrong step is the logic piece. Learn from that. Keep in mind, a missing or wrong piece does not necessarily mean that you were remiss, stupid, to blame, or that you should have known better. It only means that knowing what you know now, there was another piece available to you that logically would have had a more positive impact on you, the event, or the surrounding situation. Then use that insight in your future dealings. If it was an error in judgment, then own it, learn from it, and move on.

NOTE: A logic piece might be something done; something communicated; something changed, or discontinued, to name of few. Often SDBs are such because of a missing logic piece.

Tenet 48

Don't skip steps when you are preparing to deal with a situation or working through events. Don't miss the logic pieces. Take the time to map out the logical sequence carefully. Write the steps down for reference. If you can't clearly state each step and see how they connect logically, then you are missing pieces. Do not proceed until you have all the pieces. Do not just assume that somehow it will all work out.

NOTE: Also, always consider potential obstructions and identify contingency plans. Ask what you will do if something doesn't (or does) happen that would cause your plan to falter.

Notes

Chapter 36

Not Trying

(28)

*I*t's not hard to understand why you might decide that you've suffered enough, failed enough, or been kicked enough. That you have tried and tried and still you have not found what you are looking for. Therefore, you say, why even try? Then you stop trying. The problem is that when you stop trying, you lose your power and lower your standards. Don't settle for less—or settle for nothing. If you stop trying, you stop growing. If you stop growing, you stop living. Make not trying (especially on your worst, most painful day) never an option—ever!

Tenet 49

Don't stop trying. Slow down if you have to for a defined period of time—an hour, a day, or a week. But, don't stop. Take only a short rest to rejuvenate, reenergize, and refocus. Then jump back in. Don't wait until you feel you are absolutely ready. Start before you think you can.

Notes

PART 6

Additional Action Tools

So, where are you now? You now know you, indeed, have value. You now know you have your core. You now know where many of your feelings come from. You now know what has meaning and what doesn't. You now know what your potential is. You now know the vehicles you can use, and you also now know how to put all these concepts together to find your place. Now, I want to give you thirty-three additional tools you can use, that, added to the insights you've already gained from reading this book, can help you find control, perspective, energy, strength and value. Ultimately, they will help you find your place.

1.   Allow Yourself to Be Who You Are

It is all right to be who you are. Our tendency, sometimes, is to defend, deny, rationalize, explain, or justify what we did, what we said, what we have, or who we are—if not to others, to ourselves. We deny who we are or try to be someone we're not. This takes a great deal of time and energy and can perpetuate and deepen the pain of whatever we're dealing with, whatever we lack, and whatever we yearn for. So why expend the energy? Be okay with what you said. Accept what you did. Accept who you are.

That does not mean you won't strive to be better, and it does not mean you like whatever you might have done. It means that you did what you did and you are who you are. You know it, and you own it. It means that as you strive to be better, or for better things, you will be okay with yourself at every single point in the process—even when missteps are made. It means you will recognize and rejoice in even the small gains. Remember, it is the journey, not the destination, that is the value of life. It is the journey, not the destination, that gives your life meaning. It is the journey, not the destination, that contributes to your growth. It is from your journey, not the destination, that you will find your place.

Action: When you are in a difficult, trying, uncomfortable situation, particularly when you've done something wrong (or others think you have), assert to yourself that you are all right with who you are. You are okay with the fact that you are in a learning/growing mode, as all people are—all the time. Remember, the negatives kick your learning/growing mechanism into gear. Use the negatives and embrace them. Let them propel you forward. Be excited by the possibilities that are there as a result of the negatives—of being in the learning/growing mode. Say it—even if you don't fully feel it.

The fact is that the more you fully accept yourself for who you are, the less dependence you will have on others, or on what others do to, or say, or think about you. You also will be less emotionally damaged and paralyzed by what happens to you.

Action: When dealing with a negative event, identify the value dependency factor. "I am devastated that Cheryl left me. I feel that my value is dependent on Cheryl loving me." "If I lose the game, I'll be humiliated. I feel that my value is dependent upon winning that game." "If my boss does not like my work, I'll feel like a loser. I feel that my value is dependent upon my boss liking my work." Then, remind yourself that your value is not dependent upon or defined by any event or any person. The value dependency factor is an error in thought. Correct it.

2. Be Aware of Your Primary Triggers

Ask yourself what makes you feel the most vulnerable? Feelings of incompetence, unworthiness, embarrassment, or being low class? Feelings of being unloved, weak, poor, alone, or ugly? These are common triggers that can be pulled so easily when someone says or does something that you perceive as relating to one of them. Reactions to pulled triggers may include depression, frustration, anger, isolation, insecurity, bitterness, reactiveness, lashing out, fear, humiliation, and violence. Look out for them.

Action: At a time when no trigger is being pulled, so no emotion is present, identify, objectively, exactly what your triggers are so you can be aware when they get pulled. This recognition, itself, defuses them. You will see them for what they are: automatic, emotional, sometimes physical reactions to something done or said. Don't settle for automatic spontaneous reactions, either physical or emotional. Beware, you will experience ego rushes when these triggers are pulled particularly hard. Demand thoughtful responses from yourself—and not emotional reactions.

When a trigger is pulled, verbalize it. Say, "Because of John's comment about my menial position, my triggers about being poor have been pulled. This is about that vulnerability. Is this something I need to respond to? If so, why? Is it because by doing so I can strategically better position myself to reach my established goals? Is it to pay John back, to punish him, or convince him (or me) it's not true? If it's for strategic growth, I will respond. If not, then I will not respond or react, either physically or emotionally, because I will never react to a pulled trigger, unnecessarily. It doesn't deserve a response."

Remember, no one determines your value. Your value is absolute.

3. Find Your Core

Whenever you are faced with a negative event, whenever you feel vulnerable, self-conscious, or without value, seek out your core and engage it.

Action: Engage your core, close your eyes, breathe normally, and visualize the strands beginning to glow. Feel your strength surge inside of you.

4. Create Your Own Durable Self-Objective

A durable self-objective (DSO) is a statement that clearly identifies the kind of person you want to be. It also asks and answers how you want to be remembered. It becomes a guide, an anchor, and a compass by which you measure every one of your assumptions, perceptions, and behaviors, and it will guide you in making sound decisions. It will also help you feel secure about the person you want to be, and the person you are—especially when you are in new, unusual, or tumultuous situations. The DSO is brief, to the point, and universal. It is not relevant some of the time. It is relevant all of the time. If you stick to it and take it seriously, it will serve you well. It will guide you to your place.

Focus on three DSOs. It doesn't mean there are not other attributes you will have or work toward, but the ones you select are the ones you feel will best respond to your identified life goals and challenges (internal or external).

A DSO does not define specifically what you will do or what you will have. It defines how you will live your life and how you will respond to positive and negative situations and people in your life. Here are several examples:

Potential DSOs

- I want to be a person who people feel comfortable around.
- I want to be a person who is helpful.

- I want to be a person who is calm and controlled.
- I want to be a person who never stops trying.
- I want to be a person who takes everything in stride.
- I want to be a person who always does her best.
- I want to be a person who always sees the bright side of things.
- I want to be a person who is a good husband and father.
- I want to be a person who people come to for advice.
- I want to be a person who people value as a confidant.
- I want to be a person who is always prepared for whatever comes my way.
- I want to be a person who finishes what I start.
- I want to be a person who always responds to challenges calmly, logically, and objectively.

Action: Create your DSOs and write them down. Make copies for your wallet and your desk. Post it around your home and place a copy in your car. Read it thirty times a day—every day. You will be surprised as you begin to assume, perceive, interpret, feel, and act according to your DSO. When faced with a challenge, before acting, review your DSOs and make sure you respond according to their messages. They will anchor and guide you and your thoughts, responses, decisions, emotions, assumptions and behaviors, as you make your way through life and ultimately to your place.

5. Visualize Your Goals

How can you possibly reach or achieve something you cannot envision? If I were to tell you to bring me something I left at my home, but I did not tell you what I wanted you to get or where I live, you would most likely never find it. (How could you?) To get what you want and where you want to be, you have to know what it looks like and how to get there.

Visualization is a critical skill. It can do several things. It can help you identify and hone in on your goals. It can show you exactly what it looks like. It can guide you and it can help you focus clearly so you can get there.

Action: To visualize, identify your goal. Ask yourself what you really want? Describe it in detail. It could be tangible (money, a home, a car) or intangible (happiness). Write it down. Write down the steps you must take to make it happen. Be sure to include the very small, almost unnoticeable steps. Watch for any missing logic pieces. Identify and write down the challenges. Identify and write down how you will respond to each one. Several times a day, visualize yourself accomplishing the steps toward your goal—each and every detail.

As you visualize, consider what every one of your senses will pick up. What might you see, feel, hear, smell, and even taste? How will you think about what you experience? When you reach you goal, how will it look? What will you feel? What kinds of things will you do? How will you act? How will you spend your days getting there? Repeat this exercise often. Each time you do so, you are creating and cementing that positive vision and the motivation within you that will guide and propel you to where you want to go.

6. Select Your Personal Life Guides

We can all identify people we respect and admire for how they have led their lives and how they have, very effectively, dealt with adversity. It might be your father, your mother, a teacher, or a famous person you have never met—living or dead. It might even be a fictional character. It can be anyone you have been aware of who has dealt with life's challenges in ways you admire. You might have several personal life guides (PLG). One might be your guide for responding to threats to your ego. Another might be your guide for how to respond to business or health stressors.

Action: Select your personal life guide before acting, even before thoroughly experiencing the pain of an event. Ask yourself the key PLG question: how would your personal life guide perceive and deal with this issue? It will help to guide you and strengthen you in your own response. Be sure to reflect on your life guides during tough times. Take a moment to identify two or three people you might refer to for guidance in several different types of challenging situations. You may want to select a PLG for every DSO. Refer to the appropriate one when a challenge arises. Then ask the key PLG question: What would he/she do?

7. Do Something about It

None of what we have discussed in this book can work for you if you do not put these concepts into play. Perhaps your biggest barrier to success is simply not doing anything—becoming physically or emotionally paralyzed.

Action: When you have a challenging or an undesired task, make an agreement with yourself that you will do something about it. Then start it. Refer back to the discussion about procrastination. Staring down or avoiding such tasks or situations never resolves them. It only perpetuates the negativity they bring.

8. Do Anything Physical

We can tend to become emotionally or intellectually paralyzed and reduce our physical activities when an event or a person bothers us. Physical inaction is like having an anvil tied to our ankles and being dumped in a river. We sink lower and lower as the anvil pulls on our bodies. There is tremendous power in our ability to move our bodies purposefully during times of stress and worry. Purposeful movement increases circulation of our blood, produces endorphins, creates a healthy distraction, and creates energy. It also replaces emotional fatigue with physical fatigue, which reduces stress and the negative impact of the emotional issues. Here, we are not talking about anxiety-provoked movement e.g. pacing, or restless leg movements. Instead, we are talking about constructive movements, which include brisk walks, other exercise or creative projects with your hands.

Action: When in distress, do something physical, especially when you don't want to. Start the process. If you appear to be irreversibly stuck, in order to get the blood rushing, run, cook, sing, walk, go bowling, juggle, or dance (even by yourself, alone). Making yourself sweat is the best. When you begin to feel pulled down, move ASAP. Do it! Especially when you absolutely do not want to, even a little. In time, positive constructive physical action will become a natural response to stress.

9. Take Risks

Making positive changes in your life may require taking risks that you may have, thus far, not been willing to take. The obvious risks involve possible failure, disappointment, harm, damage, or embarrassment. The more basic, but not so obvious risks, however, are the risks of changing long-established comfortable perspectives, beliefs, philosophies, habits and engrained reaction styles. These less obvious risks, if not taken, will hold you down more assuredly than any of the obvious ones. Taking a risk does not mean acting rashly. It does not mean ignoring warning signs. It means risking not doing what your emotions are telling you to do. It means risking not doing what you usually do. It means risking being okay with making a mistake or finding that your past ways might have been wrong—at least some of the time. It also means risking being okay with waiting a little bit for your reward.

Looking back at your life on the last day you are alive, and asking why you didn't do more; why you gave up; why you did not at least try; why you didn't take a chance, are perhaps the saddest questions because they are not necessary if you take advantage of the opportunities that are out there. Risk with wisdom.

Action: At every point of critical decision-making, ask how you will feel tomorrow, next week, or next year, if you do or don't act. Should you risk not risking?

Action: Take risks that are strategic, thoughtful, measured, logical, and wise.

10.   Persist No Matter What

No matter what happens, or how you feel, get back on that horse. Giving up is never an option. If you fall off, get back on again and again and again and again. One of the hardest things to do after being thrown, but one of the most critical, is to refocus immediately on your goals (not on the event). Only when you move back to focusing on your goals and acting on them, (getting back on the horse), can you reduce the negative impact of whatever threw you.

How many times must you get back on the horse after being thrown? The answer is as many times as you get thrown. After being thrown, the very next step is to ask, "How will you try again?" Not if, but how. Then do it.

At the end of your life, you do not want to look back and say, "I gave up years ago." You want to say, "At least I never gave up."

Action: After a failure, get back on that horse, but perhaps ride it differently. Or find a different horse. Immediately plan your next strategy to try again, or, question it objectively, and adjust your direction strategically. Persist until you achieve your objective.

Action: Just do it! When faced with a challenge that has you doubting yourself. If it is inevitable that you are going to face a challenge such as making a speech or taking a test, stop and say with confidence, "I can do this." Say this without analysis, then jump in and do it. Don't worry about it. If there is no way to avoid it and no more to be done to prepare for it, just do it!

11.   Interrupting Negative Momentum – Laugh

Negative emotions carry with them a momentum that is extremely difficult to stop. Something is needed to interrupt the momentum's flow.

Action: This will sound silly, I know, but when things are going wrong—when you're angry, scared, frustrated, or sad—stop yourself and laugh or be silly. Don't look for a reason. Don't wait for the time to be right. Just laugh. Just be silly. You don't have to feel like laughing or being silly. Of course you won't, but do it anyway. Laugh deep and hard. Make silly sounds, or faces. If no one is around, laugh very loud. If there are others around, laugh quietly or be silly inside, but do it hard, and I mean deep and hard. Do it like it's the funniest thing you've ever heard. Do it every time you are faced with negative energy. You will have to force it for a while. You may have difficulty remembering to do it … But do it!

Beware, it will feel totally foreign, possibly inappropriate and contrived, but it will work. After a time, your automatic response to negative events will be to laugh Don't worry—you'll be able to keep the laughter and the silliness inside. In fact, it more likely will appear as a smile or just a positive feeling. This mobilizes you and improves your mood, improves your focus, increases your positive energy and creativity, and fires up your problem-solving skills.

If it feels too difficult, disrespectful, or otherwise, just wrong to laugh such as during times when you are mourning the loss of a loved one, then just smile, just a touch—remembering the joy your loved one gave you.

You can't laugh hard or act silly and feel bad at the same time. It interrupts the negative energy that feeds negative emotion. (Try it and you will see that this is true). It creates the positive energy you need to move yourself away from becoming stuck in the negative event and the negative thoughts and emotions that you connect with it. It also gives you the energy, perspective, and focus you need to create a new positive event.

12. Pulling Positives from the Negative

Your perception of life can be like your perception of anything else. It can be generally negative or generally positive. Considering positives in a positive light is not typically difficult. But it is particularly important to consider negatives as potential for new positives, which can be much more difficult. This practice can take you to new levels of living. Look for the positives—especially in the negatives. If a negative event is pressing heavily on you, make a point to find a potential positive event which you can use to grow and reach toward your goals.

Do not to be victimized by or act on your initial emotional reactions to negative events. If you are used to becoming hurt, angered, aggravated, or reactive to events, you may have to step back and search for the positive hiding deep inside the negative event. Then take that positive and let it propel you to your positive future and growth. This can be very different, but it can be done. For instance, you receive a bad performance review at work. The positive is that now you know exactly what you need to do to improve your next review. Now you can begin today to perform better and keep your job.

Action: At the end of each day, identify ten positive things that happened to you. If you find it difficult to name ten, stick to it until you do. You will. Big and little positives are important. Find them. If you are feeling the weight of a negative event that occurred during the day, ask how the negative is, in fact, an opportunity for future positive events. If you try, you can always find at least one example. Search for it. It may be hiding, but it's there.

Action: Let yourself enjoy your victories—even if the day is heavily burdened with negatives. Don't let even many negative events take away from the relatively few positive ones.

13. Take Responsibility

If you want something, or someone to change, remember, you always hold some responsibility to do what you can to make it happen. That doesn't mean others shouldn't change. It doesn't mean they are right and you are wrong, and it doesn't always mean you have the power to change it all on your own. But if there is something that you can control by doing something to help make the change happen, it is your responsibility to do it. Look for what you can control. That's where your focus should be. There is always something you can control—something you can impact—something you can do, maybe just a small thing. Nonetheless, that is your responsibility. You can even do something about national or worldwide events—even on a small basis. Subscribing to this concept empowers you.

Get past the idea that if you make the effort to change a wrong that is not your fault, it is somehow an admission of your own guilt, weak character, or bad judgment—or that you are too soft and are letting someone else off the hook. Get past asking why you should be the one to make the change happen when it's the other person who should change. Keep in mind, taking responsibility is not the same as taking the blame, or self-punishing, or caving in.

Taking responsibility is acknowledging that an event took place; acknowledging your role in it, if any; identifying your desired goal for the future, related to the event (what you'd like to see happen or changed); identifying what you have control over; identifying your options; and describing what you are going to do. Then act. If taking responsibility and acting gets you closer to where you want to be or helps a cause you are invested in, then why wouldn't you act?

Action: If you're dealing with a negative event, take responsibility for determining what you have control over and what you can change to make things better and work toward your goals. Then do it.

Keep in mind, control does not necessarily mean you can directly make something happen such as ending a war, or finding a cure for a deadly disease. But, you can control something that might bring about the desired response such as starting a war-ending letter-writing campaign or supporting disease research. You can control something. You can do something. But you must take responsibility to do it.

14. Squelch the Middle of the Night Angst

In the dead of night, problems tend to seem larger. An ominous threat can torture you more when there is nothing you can do about it. This is typically the case while you're lying in bed at two o'clock in the morning. It magnifies your self-perceived vulnerability and impotence.

If you can't act at that moment, let it go until you can. You might be in bed, in a meeting, or driving, You might not have access to what you need to act until tomorrow, If you can't act now, table it physically, intellectually, and emotionally. Go back to it later.

Action: During the night (or any time), if you experience angst due to something you can do nothing about at the time, table it. Say, "I'm done with this for now. I will deal with it when there is something I can do about it." If you can't do anything about a negative event and you can't shake the angst, get up immediately, smile big and laugh out loud. You won't want to, but do it. Then move. If you hope to go back to sleep, move slowly, just walk around the house calmly so you do not get your blood flowing too fast. Otherwise, shadowbox, dance, or exercise. Then go back to what you were doing. These activities interrupt negative thoughts and emotions as well as their momentum. They also foster creativity.

NOTE: Closely associated is the tendency to focus on many things at one time. Focus only on one thing at a time. If you have several major issues on your mind, work on just one of them—even if you split your time between them. When working on one, put the others aside. Then go back to the others.

15. Create a List of Abilities

So, what do you do if, in spite of everything we talked about here, you still see yourself as unable to succeed, reach your goals, or be the person you want to be? What if you cannot identify anything you are good at? "I've tried so many things, and nothing works." If this is your situation, take a step back and consider this: Human beings are equipped to do so many things well. While no one is good at everything, everyone has certain levels of capability. It is highly unlikely that an individual would not be good at anything or capable of anything.

Action: If you do feel like you are not good at anything—that nothing you do works, consider this exercise and follow these steps:

1. List the things you wish you could do that you feel you are not good at, or have not succeeded at. List them all—every one of them. Go through your entire life if you want to. Write them all down.

2. Mark with a "TR" those that you did not have all the tools/resources you needed to do them well (money, training, information, time).

3. Mark with a "C" those you really did not do everything you could have done to be successful and to do it well (lack of commitment).

4. Rate those things you want to do most with a #3; rate those you want to do less with a #2. Then rate those you want to do the least with a #1.

5. Identify those #3s you have the commitment to accomplish and mark them with a 3+.

What you have is a list of those items that are most important to you, which you also identified as having the commitment. The final step is to identify which of those items are you willing to find the resources needed to complete (if you don't already have them). This will help you to focus only on those things most important to your growth. Once you have identified those items, go for it, and don't stop until you achieve your goal.

NOTE: If you aren't willing to go all out for anything and are unhappy because of it, then you have to go back and engage your core to give you the energy and focus to identify what you want out of life and what you're willing to do to attain it. Engaging your core will do just that.

16. Become an Expert

Although it is not necessary to be expert in any area, it can help you to feel more secure if you have extensive expertise in at least one area. Expertise is knowledge. Knowledge breeds confidence. Confidence breeds energy and opportunities. Energy and opportunities breed growth. Growth breeds success and satisfaction.

Action: At the risk of sounding too simplistic, pick a topic, skill or an activity that interests you. Learn it, practice it, and use it. It does not have to be huge. It can involve work or classes, or you can learn all you can about Spain or the safety pin. Learn calculus if you want to. Learn how to juggle—really well. It does not matter. Just become an expert. Try it. Don't worry if it seems contrived. Of course it does, because it is. But knowledge and skill is knowledge and skill and again, the acquisition of knowledge and skill breeds growth, and growth breeds success and satisfaction.

17. Separate Yourself from the Noise Of The Negatives

Separating yourself from what happens to you, or around you (the noise) by engaging your core is your greatest protection. It's not running away. It's not isolating. It's taking a step back from the barrage of input, opinions, and actions of others, and then regrouping, focusing, energizing, strategizing and then acting on that which truly is most accurate and important—as determined by fact and wisdom.

Action: Step back and take a breath. If you can't separate yourself physically, clear your mind even for just a few seconds. Separate yourself from what others say, do, think and feel. Use the silence to acknowledge your value. Define yourself as whole. Find a quiet place. Pick your goal. Select your strategy. Say, "I can do this. I can handle this. I can make it through this." Then act.

Action: To separate yourself from the noise, meditate. It is not difficult. Close your eyes and breathe easy. Listen only to your breathing. Concentrate on your breathing and feel each part of your body relaxing. Your mind should be clear. Your thoughts should be quiet. No internal talking. If your thoughts begin to focus on other things, breathe a little harder or louder so you can refocus on your breathing. Do this for thirty seconds the first few times—then go to one minute, then five, and then twenty. Meditate three to five times per day—even for a couple minutes—especially when you are very stressed. It will rejuvenate you. It will help to block out the noise. It will focus you. It will rejuvenate you. There are also many meditation offerings out there—both face-to-face and on-line. Check them out.

18. Recognize Setbacks Are Tools for Growth

It is inevitable that, even after reading this book, at some point, you will suffer setbacks and, at times you might feel you are going one step forward and two steps back. It happens to all of us. Yes, all—of—us! It is too easy to let yourself become disillusioned, pulled down, frustrated, defeated and obsessed with the negatives. Keep in mind, setbacks are normal parts of life. But, beyond that, every setback is a tool for growth if you use it. Learn from it. Respond to it. In fact, they are necessary tools for growth. They spur us on. Without them, we stagnate. It may take a little time to see the growth aspect and the positive potential of a given setback, but the sooner you do, the sooner you will become energized by the negatives, not beaten by them, and the sooner you do, the sooner you will be propelled forward and not stymied by them.

For each setback, mistake, failure, disappointment, or embarrassment, immediately identify the opportunities that can result from them—learning something, starting over, changing directions, strategizing, redefining yourself, and strengthening yourself, are just a few of the potential opportunities. Search for these potential opportunities.

But, be alert, when suffering a setback, instead of paralysis, the tendency might be to plow ahead blindly, without planning or considering why or how things went awry. That's when mistakes are made. Before you jump forward, take a moment. Take a breath. Slow down. Do one thing at a time. Don't let the emotional momentum carry you away or pull you under. You might feel like you have to react to a setback immediately. Do you? Are you sure? If not, then don't. Time gives you perspective and wisdom.

Action: Except when absolutely necessary to plow ahead, when suffering a setback, recognize that setbacks are tools. Wait a minute, an hour, a day, or maybe three. Breathe. Consider how you can wisely use it and respond. Think about it. Strategize. Then respond thoughtfully and wisely.

19. Eradicate the Shadows with Light

Be alert to the shadows. Shadows are remnants of negative feelings you've felt in the past. One may creep in from time to time and try to haunt you or drag you back to a long past issue. Refocus. Play through it. Walk past it. Look beyond it.

Action: Respond to the shadows by engaging your core. Focus on your goals, note the positives, move, strategize, laugh, look to the future, and move on. When a shadow shows its ugliness, immediately upon detecting it, without thinking about it at all, engage your core and visualize its strands glowing silver and lighting up the entire area. You give the shadow no choice but to disappear. The shadow cannot survive when your core is engaged. Do not stifle the negative thought. Just allow it and then let it fade amidst the light.

20. Create a Goal-Oriented Plan

So, how do you deal with a situation you cannot avoid when you are not prepared, up to speed, or good enough? How do you deal with the resulting threat of failure?

Action: You deal with it by setting a concrete goal and making a plan. Threat of failure should breed re-assertion of goals and new planning, not ruminating over potential short-comings, or on the threat of failure. You must go through several short steps. Identify your goal for that event (be specific and concrete). Identify the challenges that may result in disappointment. Determine what you have control over. Determine a realistic goal in light of the challenges. Determine what you need to do to reach your goal. Make your plan. Write it down. Check for logic pieces. Put the plan into motion.

NOTE: Nowhere in this process do you ask who might be to blame for any potential disappointment. That answer, if there is one, is useless information. Who cares?

21. Listen for the Switch

While the mind is searching for meaning, perspective, and the reduction of stress, it can often miss, ignore, or devalue the positive relief moments—moments when you feel a little better, a little stronger, a little more in control. While many times, those relief moments are fleeting, like flipping a switch on and off, and they may be barely noticeable and quiet, they are, however, exceedingly important. Every relief moment strengthens you—even if you don't immediately feel it. It is important to recognize when a relief moment occurs and use that moment of relief to nurture and strengthen your connection with your core. One relief moment elicits another and then another. Listen for it. Look for it. Feel for it. Strengthen from it.

Action: Experience a relief moment no matter how short. Notice it. Think about how good it feels. Relish it, nurture it, remember it, and even note it in a journal. Then work toward the next one. Don't try to force them to happen. Just allow for another relief moment experience or opportunity. More will come along if you welcome each one like a good friend.

22. Deflect the Missiles

If you are like most of us, there are times during extreme situations, you might feel attacked or targeted. Even when there is no other person at odds with you, your emotions can make you feel like you are being scoped. "Why does this keep happening to me? Why is everybody always out to get me?" It is important to realize that during these times, while there may be a missile aimed at you, you can deflect it.

Example: During a very heated argument at work, you feel emotionally beaten up. When you start to react, you feel hurt, stressed, and angry—and you explode at the others in the meeting. Here, the missiles were aimed at you and hit you dead on.

You do, however, in this case, have the freedom to deflect the missiles. Freedom sits at the ready in your core. Emotionally deflecting them allows you to remain objective, independent of the situation, responsive, and strong.

Action: You must recognize that the target is separate from your core self, and you can deflect those missiles. To do so, you must engage your core. The brighter your strands glow, the more they emit power to deflect. Deflecting is a cognitive exercise that starts with you visualizing the negative things people say and do to you as bombs and then visualizing the bombs being deflected away by the power of your engaged core. Then, visualizing you walking away.

When faced with an attack, visualize those attacks as real missiles and describe them as long, sleek, bright, metallic, and heavy objects being deflected. Do this at the time they're coming down, and afterwards, as well. Visualizing the missiles makes them more tangible and limited, and it will help you respond to attacks much more objectively, strategically, effectively, and independently.

23.   Forgive the Event or the Perpetrator

We often hear about forgiving those who have wronged us in order to heal, let go of the past, reduce the pain, or focus on the future. The idea of forgiving may be hard to swallow, especially if you, or someone you care about, has been terribly wronged or harmed. But maybe not so difficult if you look at what forgiving is not.

Forgiving is not saying, "It's okay that you raped me," "It's okay that you killed my son," or "It's okay that you humiliated me." It's not saying, "I forgive you. I'm going to forget what you did to the person you hurt." It's saying, "I accept, as a reality, that it happened, and that it was you who did it. While I do not condone in anyway, what you did, I accept it as an event that did, indeed, take place, and that it had a start and an end, and now I am moving forward. Does it still hurt?

Yeah. But not to the point where it will destroy me. I can let it go to the point where I will not center the rest of my life around it or around you. I do not bind my life to it—or to you. I will no longer spend time or energy damning you or wishing you ill will. If you go on to live a full and happy life, then so be it. That's fine with me. I will not focus my life on worrying about it."

In no way do I want to over simplify these situations, or underestimate the complexities of how these events impact lives and the pain they cause. But I do want to offer this perspective because it will free you. It tells the perpetrator (and yourself) that you will not let him or her control your life. Remember, this forgiving does not suggest that you are turning your back on yourself or on someone you love or care about who was victimized by this person. It doesn't mean you don't think the perpetrator should be punished. It means you will put your life back together—completely independent of the perpetrator—so you can be there for the victim, or for others or to do good things (perhaps in honor of the person who was hurt, or yourself). To forgive is to let go.

Action: Forgive whatever or whoever haunts you. Forgiving is not forgetting. It is letting go and accepting its reality.

24.   Perform the Future Significance Test

Remember to always consider the long-term impact when gauging the level of your emotional reaction resulting from an event prior to determining your next move. If you determine that the level of emotion is too high, engage your core and scale it back.

Action: Ask if the event will be significant in a day, a week, a month, a year, or five years. Let that assessment guide you. An event that won't be significant after a week probably won't have a lasting impact and is not apt to be worth an extreme response. Though it is true, even something that has little significance in a week may be highly impactful now, and it might warrant an emotional response, don't overreact. Don't carry the emotion with you any longer than is practical or necessary.

The longer the duration of the impact, the more significant it is apt to be—and the more assertive your response should be. If you burn your dinner, the impact will only last a few minutes. No longer than it takes for you to cook something else (assuming you weren't cooking for a large formal gathering and assuming there was no fire.). No major emotional response is needed.

On the other end of the spectrum, losing your job, your freedom, a friend or loved one, or your standing certainly results in long-term impact. In response to the possible significant loss, you might respond to the event in a highly assertive manner—and with significant emotion. If the emotion is high in the case of minimal impact, recalibrate. Examine your level of emotion—rating it from one to ten, where ten is high. Then rate the significance of the event one to ten where ten is high. If the event's significance rates low and your emotion rates high, then you are over-reacting emotionally. Recalibrate. Do a quick analysis, engage your core, and balance yourself. Watch out for the ego rush.

25. Maintaining Balance

If you lean too far, you can't help but fall. That's true of all of us. If you lean, you will eventually reach the point where you can't stop yourself no matter what you do. Maintaining a balance of objective thought, motivating emotion, and goal-oriented action can keep your responses constructive, effective, and safe. It can also help you reduce excruciating pain while not denying the pain, or what is causing it. Denying the pain can cause tremendous internal pressure resulting in far greater pain when it finally is expelled. Most damage occurs when you lose this balance. The result is obsessiveness, neglect, unbridled anger, confusion, despair, rash action, or no action.

An extreme example: Terrorists maintain their intense hatred and destructiveness because over time they have lost their balance. Their emotions and behaviors have continuously gone unchecked—even energized through propaganda and training—but their intellect, their objective thought, is no longer part of the mix. As a result of the uncontrolled nature of their emotions and behaviors, lack of objective thought, and disengaged cores, they have wrapped their entire identities around their hatred and hate-filled activities. So, if they were to stop hating, they would, in fact, be nothing because that hatred and destructiveness have become their entire identity. Losing that identity would be devastating to them. It would be a loss of self, a total loss of value. So, no matter what concessions are made to them or how much damage they cause, without intensive identity-rebuilding therapy, they will never stop hating or committing destructive activities, because they would, then, lose themselves entirely. That is the ultimate loss of balance.

Action: When you feel yourself becoming extremely emotional, reactive, single-minded, or paralyzed—even if you feel you have every right and, indeed, you may be justified in feeling so, ask, "Am I balanced in my emotions, objective thoughts, and behaviors?" If not, take a step back, reconsider, reanalyze, reevaluate, and recalibrate. You should always be in balance. It starts with recognizing the imbalance. Then following some of the tenets and using the tools to respond with wisdom and objectivity.

26.   Restarting the Clock

Time always moves on. The day always ends and there is a new one ahead. Sounds almost poetic, perhaps a little saccharin. But it is true and it is a concept that must be realized, remembered, and internalized in order to ensure that you don't fall into the abyss of depression and self-deprecation, and become forever stuck and sucked down by that perpetual whirlpool of what happened yesterday. If you fully understand that fact, then any single event loses its potency and its power to keep you down because all events are time-limited and time will always pass and you can heal over time—and you know it!

Action: After every disappointment or setback, consciously start the clock over in regard to your actions, reactions, assumptions, and emotions. You restart the clock by saying, "Okay, I made a fool of myself." "I just went through a tough time." "I suffered a loss." "What will I do to craft my future, starting now?" Not, "What will I do about what happened?" Or "How will I change what happened?" Or "How will I face them?" Instead, "What will I do, starting now, about my future?" Then, start the clock again.

27. Do Something for Others

When we are faced with issues that create an ongoing state of anger, fear, defeat, despair, frustration, depression, or anxiety, the tendency can be to find ourselves in a different kind of state of imbalance. Here, we are so focused on these issues over a long period of time, that we can no longer look beyond ourselves. We can no longer look at the things that nurture our lives and give them meaning. We can no longer look at the things that give us depth, hope, and a sense of value. We, instead, focus on the one issue that is weighing heavy on us. That issue can, over time, beat us down and pull us out of balance. Inevitably, we fall.

Action: Find a way to help someone else. Help a friend or volunteer for an organization or cause. Help someone improve his or her life, or reduce his or her pain. Do something that allows you to look beyond your own position, your own pain, and your own concerns. This creates balance in your life that is critical to your own healthy functioning and to your ability to clearly identify and find your place. Do not wait until you feel better, until the time is right, or until you have solved your problem. Do it when you don't feel like doing it. Keep in mind that doing for others creates opportunities for your growth, including growth that will take you past the issue that is enslaving you.

28. Toss the Gnawing Varmint Away

Sometimes, in spite of all your efforts, something that happened or something someone said hovers over you and can't be shaken. The gnawing just won't stop.

Action: Take a moment. Engage your core. Let the thoughts that attack you go above and past you. Don't fight them. Don't ruminate on them. Don't justify yourself or attack yourself because of the thoughts you are having. Just let the thoughts pass.

To help you, visualize the gnawing thoughts coming up from behind and attacking the back of your head. Put your arms up like a football referee signaling a goal. Catch the gnawing thought and forcibly toss it to the side. As you throw the thoughts away, blow out through your mouth at the same time, blowing it out of your life. Feel the relief. If others are around or you can't use your arms, just visualize this action as soon as one of those varmints attacks you.

29. Stay Ahead of the Curve

Having a reputation for going just a little above and beyond the call of duty puts you in a position of strength and focus in the eyes of others. It also keeps you from feeling you are a pawn or a slave to the event or your life. This is because by doing this, you take control and ownership, and you determine the extent of your involvement in whatever you are facing. You deal with it assertively from a position of strength, on your own terms.

Action: Whenever you do anything, do it just a little better than what you feel is necessary or expected. This keeps you growing, keeps you in control, and keeps you energized.

30. Beware of the Single Goal

If only one thing or person will make you feel happy, safe, competent, strong, loved, relevant, significant, and worthwhile, recognize that that single-mindedness will likely cause you great heartache since there are no guarantees of success for anyone regarding any single issue or event. It also creates an imbalance that can cause you significant problems.

Action: Take a step back and consider other options that might provide the same—or similar—rewards. While still striving for the primary goal, you create balance by considering and striving for others as well.

31. Find Pleasure in the Simple Things

When times are hard, we can be so focused on our troubles and pain that we completely lose sight of the pleasures in life, particularly the simple things. In fact, it is actually your ability to recognize the beauty of the simplest things, particularly during times of great stress, that most effectively restores your balance. It is your ability to see the beauty of a flower in your yard, or in the shape of a cloud, or a kid in the neighborhood playing in the park that most effectively can release you (gives you a relief moment) from the things that haunt you.

Action: Every day, identify and write down twenty-five simple things (no less) of beauty or things that are intriguing, amusing, sweet, cool, or extraordinary in their simplicity. This will help restore your balance and engage your core.

32. Practice Brain Training

It is helpful to realize that the brain works, in some ways, like a muscle. This is not to, in any manner, suggest that biologically, the brain is a muscle. Of course, it's not. Your way of processing, to a great extent, comes from past experiences. It is learned, and since it is learned, an old way of processing can be unlearned, and a new way can be learned. What does this mean? It means you can change. It means the control is within you. It means that, with practice and effort, you can make the changes you seek.

Practicing cognitive functioning (how you think and process) can be challenging, but it can be done. Just remember, change is a process—not an event. We don't create change. We grow it and nurture it. It isn't unlike developing muscles or losing weight. It comes with time and effort. But, don't become disillusioned. While some changes can take time, many changes and their benefits begin immediately. You can bask in the glow of the large and even the seemingly very small changes. All of these bring about exceedingly powerful insights and the gains continue from the first day.

Action: Practice the cognitive changes by keeping the forty-nine tenets and these thirty-three tools in mind. Apply them consciously, particularly during times of distress. Apply them at every opportunity, especially when you do not feel like it.

33. Refuse The Ultimate Reaction

When all seems lost and life no longer seems worth living, you might consider taking your life. But before you do, ask yourself if you really want to die or just stop hurting. Typically those thinking about taking their own lives want to stop hurting and cannot think of any other way.

If you, truly, want to stop hurting, the ideas in this book will help you do just that. Recognize that even severe losses, disappointments, and failures can be dealt with. Life can go on, and there still can be good times. If you are having thoughts whatsoever about hurting yourself, seek professional help.

PART 7

Final Thoughts

So, how do you find your place in the world? It begins with recognizing what you now know to be true.

- You now know that you have a core that is invulnerable to all people and all things, and you know how to engage it.
- You now know that you have value that is undeniable.
- You now know that searching does not mean you are less than whole or defective in any way.
- You now know that you are whole because you search (not in spite of it).
- You now know that it is all right to be imperfect.
- You now know that while bad things will happen to you, it's normal, but you can overcome them.
- You now know that you have needs that are universal, and you understand them.
- You now know that the negative events in your life have no absolute significance.
- You now know that each event is short-lived, it has a start and an end.
- You now know that after one event ends, you can start a new one—a better one—with balanced thought, emotion, behavior, and infused with wisdom.

- You now know that your future is not predetermined by anyone or anything.
- You now know that you have the ability to change your decisions, opportunities, responses, directions, and priorities at any time.
- You now know that the path you take to your place is created by you—and no one else.

So where is your place? Your place is deep inside you. It is surrounded and protected by your core. In that place, you can now feel your own value—regardless of where you are, what others think, what you've done or what is happening in your life.

- You can now clearly and carefully observe and interpret the events in your life.
- You can now recognize their starts and endings—no longer haunted by past events or people or things.
- You can now, with the end of one event, start a new and better one.
- You can now make careful objective assumptions about events, and respond to them strategically.
- You can now control your life and focus on your future, your strengths, your happiness, and your growth.
- You can now act with wisdom—and not just emotion, intellect, and behavior.
- You can now balance your emotions, thoughts, and behaviors.
- You can now own your mistakes, failures, decisions, flaws, and traits without blaming yourself for them—and then put them aside once and for all.
- You can now keep your power and utilize it wisely.
- You can now enjoy your search for growth, and you can feel that growth every day.
- You can now find your place wherever you are because your place is always deep inside you—just waiting until you need it.

All of this means that you write your own script. That is absolute. While, writing your own script does not mean you can control every single aspect of your life, it does mean you can control many of them. It also means you can control your interpretations and your responses to the parts of those events you cannot control. It is up to you to write a script that will work for you.

Critical to successfully navigating your life, is to do so from a position of strength, control, vision, wisdom, and purpose.

There are many other people out there who feel exactly like you do, and they are also searching for answers and their places. So remember, you are not alone.

You now have the insights, perspectives, and skills. No one can take any of that away from you. Good luck as you continue on your exciting continual journey of growth. Your core is engaged, and you have undeniable value and wholeness. With these insights, tools, and your renewed vision, you will find your place and indeed, breathe for the first time – Gary.

Appendices

Loss and Death

I feel the need to talk more about what I think is the most severe emotional pain imaginable. The death/loss of a loved one. After such a loss, when we are left to our pain and isolation, we can easily lose our balance and our place, and find ourselves unable to breathe. What can we do with this pain? What should we do with this pain?

Along with the pain of the loss, there is an additional kind of pain. The pain that comes from the guilt of trying not to feel the pain. Of trying to lessen it. Of trying to not think about the loss. Of trying to get past it. Let me make one thing very clear. Working to get past the pain of the loss of a loved one—to avoid it, stop it, or just cope with it, in no way is indication that you want to forget your loved one, or that you don't, or didn't care enough. It also isn't true that if you do get past the pain, that you will forget your loved one. That is not what this is. This is about getting past the devastation so you can turn your thoughts to positive memories of your loved one. The fact is that you can best miss her and honor her by remembering her for her goodness and for the good times. That is the right thing to do. That's what she'd want you to do.

The torturous thoughts and feelings that can result from thinking about the one you lost, or are losing, are devastation reactions and can seem like they will never end. You may feel...

- emptiness that seems bottomless.
- like there's a hole in your heart
- breaths that catch and feel like you're suffocating, creating a sense of intense panic.
- a void from thinking about the last time you saw him, or did something with him.
- intense regret – "if only I had …"
- like your heart is being crushed by a vice.
- the need to escape into darkness.
- dread of the nighttime and darkness.
- undeserving of feeling better.
- the hollowness of realizing that she soon will be/is gone forever.
- the need to cry but afraid that you will never stop crying.
- unable to cry.
- a sense of drowning.
- dread going to bed alone with your thoughts.
- smothered with the thoughts of him.
- an ache when you find things that belonged to her.
- devastation with the firsts (the first time you go back to a restaurant that the two of you went to).
- the need to let out the pain, but not knowing how.
- you don't want to go on without him.
- waves of sadness. "I am ok for a while, then it hits me like a tidal wave."
- guilty for having moments when you do not feel the pain.
- like getting rid of his belongings is the ultimate betrayal.

There are three possibilities for dealing with this pain along with the potential results.

1. Experience that pain uncontrollably—but the uncontrolled pain can destroy you.

2. Stuff the pain so you feel nothing—but that can result in pushing the feelings of loss down so deep that at some point the pain will resurface explosively with even greater intensity.
3. Experience the pain in small doses and balance it. This allows you to fully experience your loss, which sometimes you need to do, but then balance it with a positive perspective and thoughts, and recognition of your strength.

NOTE: It is this third option that will get you through this very painful period of your life and come out of it stronger.

Allowing yourself to feel and grieve without judging yourself for doing so is critical. In fact, the pain is normal and necessary and serves a needed function. It cleanses your mind, it expels tremendous emotional pressure that otherwise can destroy you, and it signals that you need to create some balance.

Just as grieving is a natural part of the human experience that is necessary and healthy, so is our ability to continue on. We need to work with the pain and channel our grief. This is best done through balancing. Your ability to balance the pain, even for a few moments, when you do not think of the one you lost is a critical tool. You should not dread, deny, punish or apologize for it.

Remember, this does not mean you are trying to forget the one you love. It means you want to remember him or her and maintain your sorrow, but do so with a level of balance, so you can continue to live your life which is what your loved one would want.

Questions you may ask, or concerns you may have regarding the idea of moving forward after someone you love is gone, might include:

- How can I ever think of feeling better when the one I love is dying (or has died?)
- Is feeling better an indication that I no longer care and that my loved one's life no longer has significance, or that I no longer miss her?

- If I no longer hurt, will I forget him and if I don't remember him, who will?
- How can I possibly allow myself to not hurt and move on when she was so good and wonderful but is no longer here, and I am?
- Once I stop hurting, he will really be gone—and so will his significance. Will I will have robbed him of that.
- If I even try to carry on or stop hurting, aren't I betraying her?
- I am afraid that someday, if I let go of this grief, Will I forget what he looked like or sounded like.

Moving forward does not mean any of those things. It only means that without the debilitating, blinding pain, you will be able to remember him or her fully and completely.

Enjoying a moment, laughing, or reducing emotional pain is not a betrayal. You can have confidence that your love for her will not be diminished even when you don't feel the pain or think about her all the time. It doesn't require ongoing hurting and agony to prove one's love.

Your loved one's significance and your love for him or her are not measured by how much you continue to hurt from your loss. It comes from

- what you learned from her,
- what you remember of him,
- how she gave you unconditional love,
- how he made you a better person,
- what she did in her life, or
- how you use what she taught you every day.

So, what is healing? In this case, healing is being able to remember your loved one with less and less pain while being able to focus on the reasons you loved him and what you gained or how you grew because you were with him.

The pain gives you the momentum to expel the negative energy that naturally is coming from the loss. This is crucial in order to go on—and you must go on. The fact is, you are feeling the pain so intensely because your core was allowed to relax as you let your loved one get very close to you. Let's be clear, that was not an error. You want the people you love to get close. To accomplish that, you need to relax your core. We all do. With your core relaxed, your loved one can become part of you. This is the only way that you can...

- get to really know each other and understand each other;
- be connected at a deep, perhaps even spiritual level;
- feel intensely for each other; and
- share love, adoration, support, and sensitivity to each other's pleasures and pains.

This is what we want! We should cherish all wonderful relationships, but the downside is that when relationships rise to these levels, and then you experience the loss, you have to work toward reengaging your core again to reestablish yourself as whole without the one you lost. Again, this does not mean disconnecting or forgetting.

The Balance

The key is to experience the feelings, but then engage your core shortly after in order to create balance. You may have to pair the pain with emotional and mental strength. You may have to do this over and over again. You don't want to avoid thinking about the person or experiencing the pain. You want to balance it.

So exactly how do you create this balance? It starts with guiding your thoughts and feelings with channeling. You guide your thoughts through the core-engaging process and meditation. You clear your mind and allow it to rest and heal. I have described this below.

Channeling

Before the death of your loved one, if you know it's coming, anticipate some of what you are apt to experience.

- Review the devastation reactions. Work toward balance.
- Remind yourself that you are strong—mentally, physically, and emotionally—even in grief—before, during, and after the loss/death of your loved one.
- Experience the grief and your strength simultaneously.
- When your breath catches or you feel a wave of despair, experience it. Let it flow past you, then breathe normally, move, adjust, and do something constructive.
- When you feel the devastation of never seeing someone again, engage your core and remind yourself that you are strong and you are whole.
- Whenever the devastation reaction returns, engage your core.
- When you do feel a moment or two of reduced pain (a relief moment), recognize it and experience it. Enjoy it if you can. Do not question it. Do not judge yourself. It is part of the healing process.

Remember, your loved one's significance and your love for him or her are measured not by how much you continue to hurt from your loss but by what you remember and what you have gained from him:

- what you learned from her
- what you remember of him
- how she gave you unconditional love
- how he made you a better person
- what she did in her life
- how you use what she taught you every day

Remember, your goal is not to try to stop the pain, or forget your loved one. Your goal is to balance the pain with your strength by channeling the grief. Remember, when you can think of the good times, without feeling the heart-ripping pressure is when you truly honor the one you lost.

Grieve while making efforts to balance. Find ways to remember through photos or remembering times spent together.

Meditate. Through thought focusing, or thought clearing, you can allow your body and mind to rest. It can help you get through times when your negative thoughts about the person you lost are particularly painful, but you can pair the painful thoughts with positive ones to create an automatic positive thought response when the negative thoughts set in.

Find a comfortable position. Breathe normally. Feel yourself inhaling and exhaling. Listen for it. Experience it by focusing on your nostrils or your chest rising and lowering. Allow your thoughts to stay comfortably focused on your breathing. If other thoughts enter your consciousness, quietly and gently move those thoughts away and come back to focusing on your breathing.

There is no force, stifling of thought, or effort. Gently redirect your thoughts to your breathing. Allow yourself to let the negative thoughts play through or waft over you. You can focus on an object instead of your breath if that is easier for you, but make sure it holds no negative connotation or particular meaning.

Allow your mind to go blank. Whenever you think of your loved one, pair that thought with a positive thought. Identify your strengths and your future. "I will ultimately get through this, and there will be more life for me."

It is possible after meditation or any period where you focus your thoughts on more positive things, that you might feel a momentary wave of emotional pain as your thoughts return to the one you lost. Allow it, and let it flow through without fighting it. But after a couple of minutes, refocus on the positive—balance.

Tenets

Tenet 1

Life is a series of individual events. Each of them has a definite start and a definite end. Once one event ends, you start a new one. You're only bound to a past event if you allow yourself to be. Don't! And don't carry the emotion from an event that has ended into a new one that is starting. Identify each event in a challenging situation, then select a pivotal one to make a positive change. There is always at least one pivotal event. Recognize the power you have to select one and change it.

Tenet 2

The value and the reward of life is more about the searching than the outcome. The journey is more important than the destination. Celebrate the journey every day. Ask yourself, what you have learned?

Tenet 3

Allow yourself to be imperfect. Your goal is to learn and grow from your imperfections – not to avoid them. Remember, your focus is on the process – the journey. Strive, not for perfection, but for opportunities to grow. Further, you need to recognize that failure does not impede growth. It is not the opposite of success. Failure fosters action, which fosters growth, which in turn, fosters success. Finally, a failure does not indicate a lack of value. A failure is merely an event with a start and an end.

Immediately, after a failure, which is merely a negative event, plan and initiate the next event, the next step, and the next leg of your journey.

Tenet 4

The fact is that bad things are not foreign intrusions. They are integral and inevitable parts of your life and necessary for your growth. Learn and benefit from the bad things. Don't be beaten by them.

Tenet 5

Bad things will happen to you at some point, and you may feel like you are owed some good things in your life. However, life doesn't pay up just because you want it to or think it should. You have no natural right to that payment. You aren't owed anything by life. Why? Because it just isn't how life works. Stop trying to collect. Instead, jump on the back of the bad and ride it. Don't let it ride you.

Tenet 6

Every human being, at the innermost level, has a core that houses and protects their identity and value that are free and invulnerable to all things and all people. Remember that, especially during difficult times. Know it's there. Think of it. Feel for it. Visualize it. Sense it. Talk to it. Taste it. Smell it. Embrace it. Practice engaging it—often.

Tenet 7

Every behavior, feeling, or desire is intended, ultimately, to meet a basic need or is a reaction to not meeting, or potentially not meeting, such a need. When, during, or after an event, you find yourself in distress, you have to realize that the distress comes, not from the event, itself, but from a basic need level related to the event that is not being met.

This is apt to be a difficult concept to wrap your mind around, but it is a very important distinction. This will become clear as we move on through this book.

Tenet 8

During a conflict that questions your value, engage your core, and from a position of strength, attend to your basic need, not the specifics of the event. Then respond by creating a new event. Then move on to your future and your growth. Remember, never react to, draw out, or perpetuate, a negative event—create a new one.

Tenet 9

Your thoughts, emotions, and resulting behaviors are the three vehicles used to meet your needs. Your thoughts impact your emotions and your behaviors, your emotions impact your thoughts and behaviors, and your behaviors impact your emotions and your thoughts. When you are faced with emotional pain, be aware of all three—their roles, their intensity, and how each is being used during or after any given event. Be sure to keep them in balance. When you select a strategy to resolve an internal or external conflict, it is critical that you temporarily separate yourself from your emotions.

Tenet 10

If you experience negative emotions, determine if you're feeling a value or loss-triggered emotion. If it is, then engage your core. That will de-energize the emotion and detach your value, your sense of loss and your decisions from the event and those emotions. You'll be left with the motivating goal-triggered emotions that are needed to move forward.

Tenet 11

Don't act until you ask: "Why am I feeling this way and what need is being threatened?" Take the time to determine where your emotion is coming from and why? Consider the balance (or lack of balance) of thought, emotion and behavior, and identify your how you use of all three of them. Disconnect your emotion and value from the event by engaging your core. Then respond strategically and objectively.

Tenet 12

When you're emotional—either positively, or negatively—recognize the energy and momentum. No decisions should be made until the energy ebbs and the momentum stops, or at least slows. Engaging your core gives you back control and stops, or slows the momentum.

Tenet 13

Perform an OCEANS assessment. Separate the observations, cognitions, emotions, assumptions, and needs. Be sure to identify the basis of the emotion and the basic needs at risk. (Threats to your significance, value and relevance that have risen to the safety level, are often at the root, and can be particularly challenging). Engage your core, and focus less on the event and more on your needs, your future and your larger goals, then set your strategy.

Tenet 14

When things are not going well, focus inwardly. That is where you have control. Focus on your future. Don't focus on trying to change events that have already occurred, or on aspects of currently occurring events you can't change. Engage your core. Identify your basic needs at play, look to the future, and focus on what you can do now. There is always something you can do.

Tenet 15

Since events have no absolute significance or power, they cannot determine your absolute value or fate. They also don't dictate your response. Therefore, when dealing with a negative event, never focus on the event itself, or on some values-laden judgment, or assumptions resulting from it. Doing so only deepens your distress. The event happened. It's done—Period! Instead, focus on what you will do now. Focus on your future and on your growth.

Tenet 16

Differentiate between absolute significance statements and impact statements. Absolute significance statements commit you to an unchangeable status—no hope. Impact statements only identify a specific immediate result of an event that does not, by definition, predict broader implications. Deny the absolute significant statements. Use the impact statements, but only as your starting points for strategizing and taking action. An event's impact is not absolute.

Tenet 17

When faced with an event that has substantial negative impact, do not focus on the event. Do not apply absolute significance to it because there is none. Focus on its impact, but, only as a starting point for assessing the situation and strategizing your next steps toward your future and your growth. Remember that impact is not absolute either.

Tenet 18

Remember, it's never the event that determines your response. It's the thoughts, emotions, interpretations, meaning, assumptions, and needs that you wrap around that event. Make sure your information is complete, accurate, and based upon fact; that your emotions, behaviors and thoughts are balanced and carefully considered; and that your emotions are in check before you make a major decision. Do an OCEANS assessment to sort it all out. This ensures that you are clear about the entire event. Of the things you still remain unsure of, take a step back, give them a little more time, and test them out. This will help you avoid destructive outcomes.

Tenet 19

When faced with a negative event, engage your core and perform an OCEANS assessment. Be clear and accurate. Make sure your actions are based on clear observations. Make sure your thoughts are clear and ordered. Make sure you are aware of your emotions and their momentum. Make sure your assumptions are logical, based on fact, and not generalized or exaggerated. Make sure you know which of your need levels are being impacted. Reposition yourself, strategize, and act definitively but cautiously. That will keep you from choking.

Tenet 20

When faced with a decision, ask if it is right—and if it is wise!

Tenet 21

Consider how others feel about you, but only to the point where you take that information and constructively apply it with a future focus, to your own goals and plans for growth. But do so only after thoughtful consideration of the merit of the others' input. Do not to use it as proof of your value—or lack of it.

Tenet 22

The fact that others may feel you have no value due to your ineffectiveness is not part of your equation. Don't put it in there. The activities that reflect your effectiveness (or lack of it) are exclusively the tools you use to reach your goals and grow. Any negative event can help you grow if your core is engaged. Again, your value is never at stake. So, use those positive and negative events to grow.

Tenet 23

Don't demand, beg for, or expect others to give you validation or respect, or recognize your relevance, competency, or significance—in other words, your value. Don't base your actions on getting their endorsements. Work only on your goals and on your growth ... engage your core. The validation of others is apt to follow.

Tenet 24

You may demonstrate proficiency, talent, and sincerity to others—but never your value. Your value is there and does not need to be proved.

Tenet 25

If it's not imperative, let them think, say, and do what they will. If your life, job, home, or family does depend upon it, respond objectively, wisely and strategically. But don't always try to do and say the right thing simply to please others or have them give you value. Don't focus on what people think, say, or do. Focus on what you need to do now to reach your goal—to grow.

Tenet 26

Trying to undo an event typically creates more of a problem than you started with. Don't focus on the past—and certainly don't try to undo it. Instead, focus strategically on your next step toward your future.

Tenet 27

You have to be aware of whether you are reacting to substance, or an ego rush. In some cases, it can be a combination. If it is, separate the two, identify both, and attend only to the substance-based, actual, or potential practical damage.

Let them think, do, and say what they will. Keep in mind a bruised ego will try to trick you into thinking it's substantive. Don't be tricked into thinking you are experiencing—or will experience—actual damage when it isn't likely to happen. Just ask, "What can I learn from this?" Then move on.

Tenet 28

Defend—but do not become defensive. Defending defends practical goals, position, decisions, practical issues, safety, actions, people, belongings, philosophies, or principles. Defensiveness defends value. You must ask yourself: "Am I defending, or am I being defensive?"

If you are being defensive, engage your core, perform an OCEANS assessment, and stop trying to prove your value.

Tenet 29

You are whole today, you were whole yesterday, and you will be whole tomorrow. Your wholeness is there. It does not come from situations or from what people give you, feel about you, say about you, do to you, or do for you. The world does not make you whole. The world gives you unlimited opportunities for growth and ways to express your wholeness. Recognize the world as such and take the opportunities.

Tenet 30

It is the searching, itself, that makes you whole, not the result of the search. Succeed or fail. If you searched, you grew from it. You are whole.

Tenet 31

In order to deal with an error, flaw, bad decision, failure, or negative experience, own it and accept, unconditionally, that you did it. Use that complete ownership to release yourself from the event and the past, then to kick off toward your future, and move on.

Tenet 32

Embarrassment is the belief that, because of an event (your performance), others are not taking, or will not take you, seriously, or will consider you inept, silly, incompetent, or low class. When you deal with an event that causes you embarrassment, immediately engage your core and own the event, unconditionally. It is actually far easier to let go of it once you own it, than when you defend, hide it, hide from it, or beat yourself because of it.

Focus on the immediate future and say, "Okay. I screwed this up and this is what I will do to avoid similar events in the future."

Tenet 33

When faced with worry, anxiety, fear, or guilt, perform an OCEANS assessment to clearly define and sort through what is worrying you, scaring you, or making you feel guilty. Find what you can control and focus on the future. Don't pound yourself with the past. Most importantly, when those feelings arise, do something. Do not be paralyzed.

NOTE: If you are feeling guilty because you caused someone pain or injury, you must own it. Look at the issue, decide if you can make amends. If you can't then focus only on the future.

Tenet 34

Recognize that others' behaviors are simply them trying to meet their foundation needs. Don't personalize them. Try to identify what need the person is trying to meet. If you don't know for sure, just guess. I'm not suggesting you should condone the inappropriate or unjust behaviors of others. Just understand what you are seeing or experiencing. This insight gives you far more strength and control over how you respond to them—or choose not to respond to them at all.

Tenet 35

Recognize that people with problem personalities are meeting their own misguided needs, and that their personalities, their statements and behaviors are merely tools. Respond if you feel you need to, but do so from a position of strength. Stay focused on your goals—and not on the problem personality in front of you. After you say your piece, don't look back.

Tenet 36

Societal expectations are real and need to be considered, but only as guides that you consider as you make your decisions and apply your efforts toward your growth and your goals. They are not the determining factors of your identity, plan, future, or value. Your future is yours to create—and so is your plan. Remember, your value is a given.

Tenet 37

Compete with no one. Race only against yourself. Focus only on your goals—and not on your competition or the assets they have. Do this by engaging your core.

Tenet 38

When your core is not engaged, the tendency is to grab onto life clips of negative past events and then attach to your consciousness, and use them to measure your value. Engage your core to cut them loose.

Tenet 39

Reliving negative past events (replaying life clips) is a self-protecting device, but actually it does little to protect you. In reality, it reinforces the negative event and your assumptions of having less value. It keeps you stuck there, and it keeps you from focusing on your future. Engage your core—and reach to your future.

Tenet 40

Focusing on the negatives, in reality, gets you stuck on some of the most painful moments of your life. You need to seek protection, comfort, strength, and your role in life by looking at the future. Let the past go. When the negative event creeps in, own it! It happened. It started. It ended. Now move on. The more you own a past negative event (not relive it), the less pull it will have on you, and the need to search it out and relive it will be gone.

Tenet 41

Make sure you are responding and not reacting. This way, you can make sure you do not give away your power by making rash or damaging decisions. The ability to respond—and not react—is a sign of an engaged core.

Tenet 42

There are always options, but remember, two options constitute an ultimatum. Don't stop looking until you find at least three. The third one (though, in some cases, you may not like that one much, either) will free you every time. Look for it.

Tenet 43

Do not get stuck adhering to one principle if wisdom tells you something's wrong or if it results in you being miserable. When two conflicting principles are at play, infusing wisdom will help you to select the one which will minimize harm and maximize positive growth. Do not get stuck because you're scared to try something new. Ask yourself why you are standing on this principle, and look at its short-term and long-term impact. Do not let any principle force you into a life of misery or emptiness. That is not their purpose. Their purpose is to spur you on to a meaningful and rewarding existence according to your values and ethical standards. But life is not black and white. There are many nuances and variables we deal with every single day. So be sure to infuse wisdom when adhering to or selecting the most appropriate principle.

Tenet 44

A self-defeating behavior is an action that is assumed to be intended to achieve a particular goal, but (perhaps unconsciously) it meets another more immediate goal. It may actually create a larger barrier to achieving the assumed intended goal, or it may achieve the assumed intended goal, but cause other problems in other areas.

It is up to you to recognize your own SDB and the opposing forces at play. You must determine what need it is meeting and how it is meeting it. If it isn't working—or if it is but it is also causing other problems—find another behavior that will be more effective in the short term, as well as the long term. Separate your decision from all emotion. Don't give in to the short-term reactive fixes, even if they are, in some way, absolutely justified unless you've thoroughly evaluated all aspects of the potential impact—both short-term and long-term. This process can be helpful for understanding and responding to others' SDBs as well, thereby reducing the chances that you will be hurt by it down the road. All this will help you find your place.

Tenet 45

Don't become emotionally paralyzed. Think, plan, and respond—but do so strategically and not rashly, reactively, or vindictively. If you choose not acting as your strategic response, be sure it will really take you where you want to go.

Tenet 46

Remember, old undesirable roles can creep back into your life. Don't be drawn into filling them. Respond to role regulation from your current role—and not from the old one that is long gone.

Tenet 47

Procrastination is a vehicle intended to meet an immediate need via a quick fix, at the expense of more important, more significant, larger, or longer-term needs, goals and implications. When faced with the potential that you might procrastinate, focus on the potential longer-term negative impact that will result from procrastinating and visualize the impact in detail and the feelings you will have if you don't get it done now. Then, plan the completion of the activity the night before you are to start it. Visualize it in detail. Then agree to just start it.

When you do so, if it can't be practically and realistically completed right away—or you are just compelled to do something else—select an amount of work from the task at hand you will complete at that sitting. Go a small distance (five minutes or one or two steps) beyond where you thought you would originally stop. This will mobilize and energize you without overwhelming you. Then plan your next effort toward completion.

By continually selecting a goal for each sitting, then progressing just a few steps further, it will stretch your ability to address the task while not putting such great pressure on you to the point where even thinking about it, causes you to put it off. It will put you back in the driver's seat—not being directed by the forces of procrastination. It will also result in your getting at least a little more done. If you agree to do five more minutes than the plan stated, do the five and then two more.

Tenet 48

Don't skip steps when you are preparing to deal with a situation or work through events. Don't miss the logic pieces. Take the time to map out the logical sequence carefully. Write the steps down for reference. If you can't clearly state each step and see how they connect logically, then you are missing pieces. Do not proceed until you have all the pieces. Do not just assume that somehow it will all work out.

Tenet 49

Don't stop trying. Slow down if you have to for a defined period of time—an hour, a day, or a week. But, don't stop. Take only a short rest to rejuvenate, reenergize, and refocus. Then jump back in. Don't wait until you feel you are absolutely ready. Start before you think you can.

About the Author

Gary is the CEO of Transitions Mental Health Services in Rock Island, Illinois. Gary graduated from the University of Iowa with a master's degree in social work and is a licensed clinical social worker. Gary also teaches master's classes at St. Ambrose University in Davenport, Iowa, on a variety of topics related to the field of social work. Gary served as the president of NAMI-IL (National Alliance on Mental Illness) in addition to serving on a variety of committees focusing on ensuring the health and well-being of people with mental health problems.

Over the past thirty years, Gary has provided therapy, counseling, and consultation to individuals with mental health issues, including mental illnesses, personality disorders, behavior disorders, and issues negatively impacting the lives of those he serves, as well as consultation to their families and friends and others who care about them. Gary has also provided trainings and consultation to businesses, educators, and social services providers on a variety of topics, including mental disorders, the mental health system, vocational rehabilitation, and coping with, living with, serving, and responding to individuals with challenging behaviors.